Penguin Masterstudies

KW-052-562

A Passage to India

Roger Ebbatson is Senior Lecturer at Worcester College of Higher Education. He studied at the universities of Sheffield and London and taught at colleges in London before moving to the University of Sokoto in Nigeria. He is the author of a number of articles on nineteenth-century and twentieth-century English literature and of two books, *Lawrence and the Nature Tradition* (1980) and *The Evolutionary Self: Hardy, Forster, Lawrence* (1983). He has also contributed a study of *The Mill on the Floss* to the Penguin Masterstudies series and has edited Thomas Hardy's *A Pair of Blue Eyes* and *The Trumpet-Major* for Penguin Classics.

Catherine Neale was educated at Newnham College, Cambridge, and the University of Edinburgh. She has taught at the Open University, the University of Edinburgh and the Extramural Department of the University of Birmingham. She is currently Lecturer in English at Worcester College of Higher Education.

Penguin Masterstudies
Advisory Editors:
Stephen Coote and Bryan Loughrey

E. M. Forster

A Passage to India

Roger Ebbatson and Catherine Neale

Penguin Books

Penguin Books Ltd, Harmondsworth, Middlesex, England
Viking Penguin Inc., 40 West 23rd Street, New York, New York 10010, U.S.A.
Penguin Books Australia Ltd, Ringwood, Victoria, Australia
Penguin Books Canada Limited, 2801 John Street, Markham, Ontario, Canada L3R 1B4
Penguin Books (N.Z.) Ltd, 182–190 Wairau Road, Auckland 10, New Zealand

First published 1986

Made and printed in Great Britain by
Richard Clay (The Chaucer Press) Ltd, Bungay, Suffolk
Filmset in Monophoto Times by
Northumberland Press Ltd, Gateshead, Tyne and Wear

Contents

Acknowledgements 7
A Note on the Text 9
1. Biographical Sketch 11
2. Forster's Ideas 16
3. The British in India 29
4. Forster's Involvement with India 33
5. The Composition of the Novel 38
6. The Title of the Novel and a Synopsis 40
7. Commentary and Analysis 44
   Themes and characterization (CN) 44
   The authorial voice (RE) 59
   Structure (CN) 73
   The symbolism of the novel (RE) 78
   Comedy and irony (CN) 91
   The colonial encounter (RE) 98
   The critical reception of the novel and
     varieties of interpretation (CN) 113
8. Appendix: Forster's other novels 123
   Select Bibliography 138

Acknowledgements

Passages quoted from the text of *A Passage to India* are published by permission of Edward Arnold Ltd.

A Note on the Text

All page references to *A Passage to India* are to the Penguin Modern Classics edition edited by Oliver Stallybrass (Penguin Books, 1979, reprinted in Penguin Classics, 1985).

Page references to other works by Forster are to the following editions: *Abinger Harvest*, Penguin, 1967; *Aspects of the Novel*, Penguin, 1976; *The Hill of Devi*, Penguin, 1965; *Howards End*, Penguin, 1967; *The Longest Journey*, Penguin, 1960; *Maurice*, Edward Arnold, 1971; *A Room with a View*, Penguin, 1978; *Two Cheers for Democracy*, Penguin, 1965; *Where Angels Fear to Tread*, Penguin, 1959.

1. Biographical Sketch

E. M. Forster was born in London on New Year's Day 1879. His father, a London architect, was associated with the reformist and evangelical Clapham Sect. When Forster was only two years old, his father died. In consequence, the boy was brought up entirely by three women: his great-aunt, Marianne Thornton, an affectionate but dictatorial woman; his witty maternal grandmother, Louisa Whichelo, and his mother, Alice Clara Forster, *née* Whichelo, known as Lily. Forster's mother was the daughter of a poor drawing-master, and had herself been brought up by Marianne Thornton. She was to be a dominant influence upon Forster's life; indeed, he lived principally with his mother until her death in 1946, when the writer was sixty-seven. Marianne Thornton died in 1887, when the child was eight, and left him a legacy of £8,000, the interest from which would later enable Forster to live without paid employment. 'She and no one else made my career as a writer possible,' he was to note in his biography of Marianne, 'and her love, in a most tangible sense, followed me beyond the grave.' (The sense of a person living through others was to become a crucial aspect of Forster's fiction, for instance in Mrs Wilcox of *Howards End* or Mrs Moore in *A Passage to India*.) The Whichelos were always associated in Forster's mind with love, culture and improvidence, values which he set against the 'public activity, private benevolence' of the Clapham Sect. After the death of her husband, Mrs Forster retreated into the countryside and rented a house called Rooksnest in a still rural Hertfordshire. It was in this old house, with its adjacent farm and massive wych-elm, that the boy grew up. The house took on a symbolic value for Forster, representing to his mind a vital English tradition. It became an image of what F. R. Leavis called Forster's 'elemental hunger for continuance', a 'hunger' to be most powerfully expressed in his novel, *Howards End*. It was at this time that a youthful Forster befriended a garden-boy called Ansell, an episode which was to presage the many close relationships (usually male) between different classes and cultures in Forster's fiction. When Forster was approaching his teens, the family was evicted from Rooksnest. 'If I had been allowed to stop on then,' Forster ruminated fancifully later, 'I should have become a different person, married, and fought in the war.' Instead, at the age of eleven, Forster was sent to an undistinguished prep school at Eastbourne, and thence to Tonbridge School as a day-boy, his mother residing in the town. At Tonbridge School Forster experienced deep unhappiness: he hated the conventional values of the public school system, with its pressure to conform, and its stifling of the imaginative and emotional life of the individual boy. The impact of this environment was to be devastatingly recreated in the portrayal of Sawston School in Forster's second novel, *The Longest Journey*. Such an education, Forster came to believe, produced 'well-developed bodies, fairly developed minds, and undeveloped hearts' – features typified, for instance, in the characterization of Ronny Heaslop. Forster's deliverance from this ordeal came in 1897 when he went up to King's College, Cambridge; he was to be associated with both college and city for the remainder of his long life. He took a Second in the Classics Tripos in 1900, and then switched to History in 1901. Academic attainment was not, however, Forster's goal. Under the idiosyncratic tutelage of Nathaniel Wedd, his classics tutor, Forster gained a love of modern literature, a hatred of authority and a reverence for the Greek ideal of male comradeship. With friends such as Goldsworthy Lowes Dickinson and H. O. Meredith, Forster abandoned conventional Christianity completely. He recalled the idyllic period when he was invited to join the 'Apostles' debating society:

As Cambridge filled up with friends it acquired a magic quality. Body and spirit, reason and emotion, work and play, architecture and scenery, laughter and seriousness, life and art – these pairs which are elsewhere contrasted were there fused into one. People and books reinforced one another, intelligence joined hands with affection, speculation became passion, and discussion was made profound by love.

Forster's generation, many of whom were later to become members of the metropolitan 'Bloomsbury Group', were deeply influenced by the ideas of the philosopher, G. E. Moore, whose *Principia Ethica* (1903) advocated the supreme value of art, beauty and personal relations. The heady atmosphere of this period of Forster's life is recreated in the opening Cambridge scenes of *The Longest Journey*. To Forster, the muddle and mystery of England was neatly symbolized by the courtyard of King's College and its magnificent chapel:

Gibbs's Building is pierced by a cavernous entry, known to initiates as the Jumbo House, in whose sombre recesses are usually to be found a ladder, a hand cart, and a small heap of sand. These too are peculiar to England. The range from them to the soaring chapel buttresses, pinnacled in the intense inane, is the range of the English mind. They are the unexplained, balancing the inexplicable.

In a sense, these days at Cambridge were the high point of Forster's life. After going down from the university, he spent some years in desultory work and travel. During 1902 he taught for a while at a Working Men's College, and travelled in Italy and Greece, countries he always loved deeply. In 1905 he took on the post of tutor to the children of the Gräfin von Arnem, an English woman who had written the popular *Elizabeth and her German Garden* some years earlier. After this entertaining interlude, Forster returned to the maternal home at Weybridge in Surrey. It was at Weybridge in 1906 that he first met a young Indian, Syed Ross Masood, who came as a pupil but was to become a lifelong friend, and part model for Dr Aziz. Forster had been writing short stories since the early years of the century, and he published his first novel, *Where Angels Fear to Tread*, in 1905. A more autobiographically based novel, *The Longest Journey*, followed in 1907, and *A Room with a View* the following year. *Howards End*, his first major success, was published in 1910. Following this literary advance, Forster made, during 1912 and 1913, a major geographical advance by travelling to India with his friends, Lowes Dickinson and R. C. Trevelyan. Far more powerfully than Italy and Greece, India helped Forster to place the suburbanism and narrowness of English society in a wider context. By this stage of his life Forster was an accepted and admired member of the Bloomsbury Group, many of whose members he had known at Cambridge. The group, though heterogeneous, evidently shared the values of aesthetic beauty and personal companionship which Forster's work always endorsed. It included such diverse talents as Virginia Woolf, the novelist; her sister Vanessa Bell; the artists Duncan Grant, Clive Bell and Roger Fry; Lytton Strachey, the witty biographer; Leonard Woolf, a journalist; and John Maynard Keynes, who was to become one of the most influential economic theorists of the twentieth century. A historian of the Bloomsbury Group finds within the circle 'a common respect for things of the spirit', a belief in the supremacy of 'the inner life' and an admiration for 'tolerance and honesty'. He continues, in words which are certainly applicable to Forster:

the integrity and careful composition of their books demonstrate a profound respect for art, and a conviction that form is as important to a work of art as content; that, indeed, the two are inseparable since the artist cannot express emotions and ideas adequately except in significant form.

The group had no formal status, and has been neatly characterized as a 'tendency' rather than a club. The tendency would include an agnostic view of religion, responsiveness to modern art, and liberal sympathies in politics. Forster was aptly enough to describe himself later as belonging to the 'fag-end' of the liberal tradition. Many of the group took a pacifist line during the Great War, but Forster served with the Red Cross in Alexandria from 1915 to 1918. Before the outbreak of war, he composed a secret novel, *Maurice*, in which for the first time in fiction he expressed something of his own homosexual nature. This novel was circulated among friends who Forster felt would be sympathetic. The writer experienced his first genuinely fulfilling sexual relationship when he met a tram-conductor in Alexandria. After the events of the war, Forster returned to India in 1921 to act as secretary to the Rajah of Dewas State Senior, one of the smaller Indian native states. His often hilarious experiences were to be described in *The Hill of Devi*, published in 1953. At a more profound level, the journey back to India compelled Forster to return to the idea he had formulated after his first visit, of a new novel set in the sub-continent. He worked on what became *A Passage to India* on his return to England, helped and encouraged in what was a painful gestation period by Virginia and Leonard Woolf. The book was finally published in 1924 to wide acclaim. For the remaining forty-six years of his life, Forster was to publish no more novels, partly because of the difficulties he encountered in dealing openly with homosexual themes. On his return to England, Forster continued to live with his mother at Abinger Hammer in Surrey, but he liked to escape from the maternal atmosphere occasionally, and rented a flat in London where he could enjoy the company of homosexual writer friends such as J. R. Ackerley and William Plomer. Although Forster's career as a novelist effectively came to an end in 1924, he became increasingly active in the public sphere, where he was seen as a symbol of the liberal conscience. In 1927 he delivered the Clark Lectures at Cambridge, which were to become *Aspects of the Novel*, and he was made a Supernumerary Fellow of King's College until 1933. The following year he was elected first president of the National Council for Civil Liberties. His collections of essays,

Abinger Harvest (1936) and *Two Cheers for Democracy* (1951), are often concerned with explorations of his liberal position in politics and the arts. Forster made a number of broadcasts for the BBC during the Second World War, and here again he utilized the new medium to ruminate upon the nature and demands of civilization. He retained a lively interest in the affairs of India, and returned to the sub-continent in 1945, two years before independence. In 1946, on the death of his mother, Forster left Surrey and returned permanently to King's College, Cambridge. At this time he began his important connection with the Aldeburgh Festival in Suffolk, run by Benjamin Britten and Peter Pears. In 1951 Forster provided the libretto for Britten's opera, *Billy Budd*, based on the story by Herman Melville. Forster led a peaceful and happy life in his beloved Cambridge, and his last years were marked by increasing public recognition. In 1953 he was made a Companion of Honour, and in 1969 he was awarded the prestigious Order of Merit. After E. M. Forster's death in 1970, *Maurice* and *The Life to Come*, both dealing primarily with homosexual subjects, were finally published.

2. Forster's Ideas

Forster once said:

> I belong to the fag-end of Victorian liberalism, and can look back to an age whose challenges were moderate in their tone, and the cloud on whose horizon was no bigger than a man's hand. In many ways it was an admirable age. It practised benevolence and philanthropy, was humane and intellectually curious, upheld free speech, ... and entertained a sincere faith in the progress of society. ('The Challenge of Our Time', 1946, *Two Cheers for Democracy*, p. 65)

Forster is often called a 'liberal humanist'; a term for a way of thinking which is characteristic of the years between 1900 and 1914. His liberalism is in the tradition of the great Victorian liberal thinkers such as Matthew Arnold, who sought to combat industrialism and materialism through an emphasis on culture, and by arguing the benefits to society of educating people to be sensitive, enlightened and cultured. For Forster, this intellectual trend was confirmed by the work of the philosopher, G. E. Moore, whom he knew at Cambridge. In *Principia Ethica*, published in 1903, two years after Forster went down from Cambridge, Moore argues that what matter are states of mind, not necessarily connected with action, and that brutal action can never be justified. The logical conclusion is, and was for Moore, that the ultimate values are love and beauty, to be pursued and found in the enjoyment of personal relationships and in the appreciation of art. This conclusion is what appealed to the Bloomsbury Group, and, of course, to Forster. He himself defined the humanist in an essay on André Gide, in 1943: he says, 'The humanist has four leading characteristics – curiosity, a free mind, belief in good taste, and belief in the human race' ('Gide and George', *Two Cheers for Democracy*, p. 231).

The claims made by liberal humanist thinkers for art, culture, subjectivity and personal relations are based on a faith in human nature, in the integrity of the individual, and in the significance of culture and the individual's actions for the wellbeing of society. Forster's faith in the individual is not so much socially based – he does not define human beings in terms of their social role and function, for example – as deriving from the observation that human beings not only have a social dimension but also a spiritual, intensely private dimension, that sometimes he calls the 'soul'. This belief in spiritual capacity was fostered by his friendship with, and reading of, Edward Carpenter, who for many years argued that human beings have great potential for wholeness and fulfilment, if they could but discard the crippling effects of 'civilization' and regain a meaningful relationship with nature.

Forster's novels emphasize the importance of a feeling heart, of personal relationships, tolerance and good will. This is often linked with a mystic faith in the beneficence of nature and in the instinctual side of human beings. Throughout his novels, Forster also satirizes what he perceives as the enemies of these qualities: the philistinism and materialism of the English middle class, which he frequently identifies with the public school ethos, and which he suggests has disastrous effects on the individual, and, by implication, on society.

'Liberal humanism' extended the liberal ideas of the Victorian intelligentsia, but it was also a reaction against other Victorian tendencies to deny individual impulse and spontaneity in the interests of authority and social institutions. There were, however, strains implicit in it as a model for individual behaviour during those years prior to the Great War. There was a growing feeling that the stability and security of England were being eroded by the increasing pace of twentieth-century life. However, it was not until 1914, with the onset of the Great War, that liberal-humanist values, and an emphasis on love and beauty, were felt to be relatively powerless to confront the wider historical and political currents in life. The Great War, and subsequent historical events and political developments, have all imposed an irony on a 'humanism' such as Forster's.

Forster himself was well aware of the contradictions of his beliefs, which are focused most urgently in *A Passage to India*, the only novel of his to be written after the Great War. It is possible to argue that Forster's early work expresses a fairly secure faith in liberal humanism, in the way that it portrays the importance of personal relationships and beauty and satirizes those enemies Forster discerns in the English establishment. *Howards End* (1910) begins to betray the recognition that such values are only significant in a personal arena, and *A Passage to India* extends this observation. This way of describing the shifts in Forster's ideas and fiction relies on the argument that external events disproved certain long-held convictions about human nature and its efficacy in social life: the Great War 'happened', and liberal humanism died a strange death. Forster certainly agreed with this analysis, saying that

Matthew Arnold's 'bad days' are Halcyon when compared with our own. He belonged to an age which was concerned with problems of faith, doubt, and personal survival; he was worried by these, but the collapse of all civilization, so realistic for us, sounded in his ears like a distant and harmonious cataract... We are passing through a much rougher time, perhaps the roughest time that has ever been. And if we look back into the past for comfort, we see upon the faces of its great men a curious mixture of comprehension and of blankness. ('A Note on the Way', 1934, *Abinger Harvest*, p. 85)

Apart from a few short stories, Forster wrote no more fiction after *A Passage to India*, but he wrote a great deal of criticism and commentary on the spirit of the times which he found himself living through. The essays in *Abinger Harvest* (1936) and *Two Cheers for Democracy* (1951) consistently place the values he had always espoused against external and impersonal developments: bravely and firmly, but with a sense of resignation. The fundamental belief that he returns to again and again is his faith in the individual:

I have no mystic faith in the people. I have in the individual. He seems to me a divine achievement and I mistrust any view which belittles him. If anyone calls you a wretched little individual – and I've been called that don't you take it lying down. You are important because everyone else is an individual too – including the person who criticizes you. In asserting your personality you are playing for your side. ('The Challenge of Our Time', *Two Cheers for Democracy*, p. 66)

It is this that had led him, in 1939, to make the famous statement, 'I hate the idea of causes, and if I had to choose between betraying my country and betraying my friend, I hope I should have the guts to betray my country' ('What I Believe', *Two Cheers for Democracy*, p. 76). In the same essay, though, he gives democracy 'two cheers' because it 'admits variety and ... permits criticism. Two cheers are quite enough: there is no occasion to give three. Only Love the Beloved Republic deserves that' (p. 78). In his later essays, Forster also upholds the value of art in the world:

Art is valuable not because it is educational (though it may be), not because it is recreative (though it may be), not because everyone enjoys it (for everybody does not), not even because it has to do with beauty. It is valuable because it has to do with order, and creates little worlds of its own, possessing internal harmony, in the bosom of this disordered planet. ('The Challenge of Our Time', *Two Cheers for Democracy*, p. 68)

Here the feeling of being under attack from the external forces of violence and disorder is very strong. And Forster's lifelong rejection of industrialism also becomes, in later years, a denunciation of what has already happened, which he is relatively powerless to prevent:

there is a huge economic movement which has been taking the whole world, Great Britain included, from agriculture towards industrialism. That began about a hundred and fifty years ago, but since 1918 it has accelerated to an enormous speed, bringing all sorts of changes into national and personal life. It has meant organization and plans and the boosting of the community. It has meant the destruction of feudalism and relationships based on the land, it has meant the transference of power from the aristocrat to the bureaucrat and the manager and the technician. Perhaps it will mean democracy, but it has not meant it yet, and personally I hate it. ('English Prose between 1918 and 1939', 1944, *Two Cheers for Democracy*, p. 278)

Forster, then, bears witness to the historical problems for the liberal-humanist thinker. His writing criticizes the shortcomings of such a personal emphasis within the public world, but also upholds the sovereignty of the claims of the personal. Many readers value Forster for his lifelong integrity; W. W. Robson, for example, says, 'If words like "liberal" and "civilized" and "tolerant" can still be used unironically, it is largely because of the work of this quiet, unpretentious, witty writer.' And Noel Annan wrote in the *Observer* in April 1985:

Forster's novels and essays make it clear who his enemies were: the pompous officials, the intolerant know-alls, the prudes and the snobs who treated people from a different class or race as inferiors; and it is a measure of his influence that for some years now decent men and women have thought that to be like them is intolerable.

On the other hand, some readers choose to emphasize the ironic, and even discouraged, side to Forster's statements. Lionel Trilling claims that Forster is 'at war with the liberal imagination'; according to Trilling, the liberal tends to view human beings as either good (i.e. sensitive, emotional and imaginative), or bad (snobbish, intolerant and repressed), but Forster portrays them as 'good-and-evil'. There is, says Trilling, an essential irony in Forster's writing which defuses a typical liberal tendency to complacency.

19

Liberal humanism is not a defined philosophy, but rather a way of thinking, and in that sense it is an ideology. While he may adopt an ironic stance to some of the pitfalls of liberal humanism, Forster never seriously questions the assumptions underlying it as a mode of thought. But as well as there being historical problems for liberal humanism since the Great War, there are also ideological problems. It is worth mentioning these here, in order that Forster's own unquestioned assumptions become evident to the reader. An emphasis on art and personal relations, beauty and love, relies on certain ideas about the nature of the individual: for example, that there is an undefinable, private element within us all, that we may call the 'soul', and that we are, therefore, agents of free will. Some critics, especially some Marxists, would argue that the individual, or the 'subject', is defined in terms of social, political, material and historical forces, and that the claim that the individual has personal autonomy confers an illusion of freedom on the individual, which does not actually exist. If the human being has a 'soul', then ideas of good and evil, and the possibility that human nature can be intrinsically good, are available: a great deal of modern thought and analysis questions this assumption. For example, the ideas of Marx, Nietzsche and Freud all offer, in different ways, the insight that subjectivity is a site of oppression and violent impulse as well as of creativity and spontaneity. Forster quite consciously drew back from the implications of this kind of insight:

... Psychology has split and shattered the idea of a 'Person', and has shown that there is something incalculable in each of us, which may at any moment rise to the surface and destroy our normal balance. We don't know what we are like. We can't know what other people are like. How, then, can we put any trust in personal relationships, or cling to them in the gathering political storm? In theory we cannot. But in practice we can and do. Though A is not unchangeably A or B unchangeably B, there can still be love and loyalty between the two. For the purpose of living one has to assume that the personality is solid, and the 'self' is an entity, and to ignore all contrary evidence. And since to ignore evidence is one of the characteristics of faith, I certainly can proclaim that I believe in personal relationships. ('What I Believe', *Two Cheers for Democracy*, pp. 75–6)

Finally, Forster's emphasis on individualism and the personal prejudges the relationship between the individual and the society in which he or she lives; instead of the possibility of direct intervention or action, the individual is perceived as passively influencing the development and progress of society – or, of course, *not* influencing it when events overwhelm the realm of the personal. It is in this sense, for example, that Arnold Kettle criticizes *A Passage to India* for revealing Forster's failure to assess 'the capacity of human beings radically to change their consciousness'.

At this level, and in this sense, Forster never expresses a fundamental dissatisfaction with liberal humanism as a model for human behaviour. His authorial voice is present everywhere in his fiction, and creates a collusion with the reader in liberal-humanist values, however much those values may be locally questioned. His style is confident, humorous and wise, and it is worth noting at this point that while it is attractive and even flattering to the reader, it too carries certain assumptions that we may, in the end, not always agree with.

In 1913, while visiting India for the first time, Forster shared a picnic with some Anglo-Indians:

Mrs Gamlen. 'What sort of novels do you write? Are they nice?' *Forster.* 'I can answer that no.' *Mrs G.* 'Oh I see, they are modern?' *F.* 'Yes, that is the alternative.' *Mrs G.* 'Problem novels, I suppose. Well for my own part I think there are no problems left they have all been written about.' *F.* 'Yes, they are old, but the writer's young.'*

Forster's novels are *not* nice, and he was always ambivalent about the conventional demands and themes of the realist novel. With its characteristic interest in personal relations and social and moral concerns, the realist novel is in many ways a product of the liberal-humanist stance; however, it is as if Forster does not wish to subscribe wholeheartedly to the referential realism of the novel as a form. In many ways, he modifies the conventional topics. He wishes to write about people and so creates, on the whole, plots of education, love and marriage. But in his novels, coincidences, sudden and unexplained deaths, and violence abound. His ambivalence about the degree to which the novel can give the impression of verisimilitude is marked when he comments, in *Aspects of the Novel* (pp. 62–3),

The constant sensitiveness of characters for each other ... is remarkable, and has no parallel in life, except among people who have plenty of leisure. Passion, intensity at moments - yes, but not this constant awareness, this endless readjusting, this ceaseless hunger.

Forster's novels are unsettling to the reader for a number of

---

*Quoted by P. N. Furbank, *E. M. Forster: A Life* (OUP, 1979), I, p. 252.

reasons. They combine social comedy in the tradition of Jane
Austen, with poetic and visionary elements. As well as characterization and plot, there is considerable recourse to symbolism and
mysticism; indeed, as John Beer says, 'The reader who relies on plot
alone will be left with nothing concrete to grasp when he lays down
the novel.' Frequently the tensions between these different kinds of
fictional writing become evident in the endings of the novels, which
display both symbolic and realistic strategies for terminating the
concerns and themes of the novels. Forster often adopts a direct,
non-realistic authorial voice, adding a dimension of his own ideas
and beliefs to the fictional devices of narrative, plot structure and
characterization.

Aspects of the Novel, the published version of a course of lectures
given by Forster at Cambridge in 1927, demonstrates Forster's
characteristic liberal-humanist frame of mind, and his own ideas
about the novel as a form and about writing novels. Indeed, the
book is of interest more because of what it illustrates about Forster
than because of his comments on novels by other writers, which are
often idiosyncratic and sometimes flippant – Sir Walter Scott and
Henry James, for instance, are hardly discussed in the spirit of
disinterested inquiry, but are berated for shortcomings relevant to
Forster's own preoccupations.

Forster's tone in the book is colloquial and witty, reflecting his
claim that he is an amateur critic and that his course of lectures is
'ramshackly'. He disclaims any pretensions to what he calls 'pseudo-
criticism', for,

Books have to be read (worse luck, for it takes a long time); it is the only
way of discovering what they contain. A few savage tribes eat them, but
reading is the only method of assimilation revealed to the West. The reader
must sit down alone and struggle with the writer, and this the pseudo-
scholar will not do. (*Aspects of the Novel*, pp. 30–31)

With an emphasis on reading the books, and a distrust of theoretical
approaches to a discussion of the novel, Forster's criterion for
judgement and evaluation is predictable: the human heart, for 'The
final test of a novel will be our affection for it, as it is the test of our
friends, and of anything else which we cannot define' (*Aspects of
the Novel*, p. 38). For Forster, the novel is primarily important
because of its close connection with humanity and with human
aspirations and failings. The author's power is in revealing inner
feelings; the novel is valuable because it offers readers what all

human beings hanker after – understanding of life and an illusion of permanence. This emphasis on emotion and feeling is extended when Forster considers characters and characterization. In several highly-charged passages, Forster describes the isolation of being human; for example:

> human intercourse, as soon as we look at it for its own sake and not as a social adjunct, is seen to be haunted by a spectre. We cannot understand each other, except in a rough and ready way; we cannot reveal ourselves, even when we want to; what we call intimacy is only a makeshift; perfect knowledge is an illusion. (*Aspects of the Novel*, p. 69)

The beauty of fictional characters, and the appeal of the novel as a form, are that we can 'know' the people in books, says Forster. 'They are people whose secret lives are visible or might be visible' (*Aspects of the Novel*, p. 70), whereas human beings have invisible secret lives. It is the function of the novelist to reveal those secret lives – not through action, but through his or her knowledge of the characters: 'the writer can talk about his characters as well as through them, or can arrange for us to listen when they talk to themselves' (*Aspects of the Novel*, p. 85). Consequently, 'round' characters are satisfactory in Forster's opinion precisely because they convince us that they might be human beings, as well as being more knowable than human beings; 'The test of a round character is whether it is capable of surprising in a convincing way' (*Aspects of the Novel*, p. 81).

This emphasis on the 'humanity' of the novel, which is so true to Forster's liberal-humanist priorities, results in a feeling of the unmanageability of the novel form, bursting with characters and life. And Forster's belief in the permanence and timelessness of art is expressed by him as a conflicting claim of the novel form. He envisages the plot as a kind of higher government official, requiring individuals (i.e. characters) to contribute to 'higher interests'. In this comic vein, the struggle appears to be fairly equal, but Forster's first loyalty is to the disordered air of humanity available in the novel, for 'Human beings have their great chance in the novel' (*Aspects of the Novel*, p. 149).

However, much of *Aspects of the Novel* stresses the importance of technical care and the *art* in writing. Plot, according to Forster, 'ought to be economical and spare; even when complicated it should be organic and free from dead matter' (*Aspects of the Novel*, p. 88).

From this aspect comes the element of beauty which we discern in a novel as art-form, and the apprehension of beauty increases in Forster's mind when he comes to discuss 'pattern' and 'rhythm', pattern being 'the book as a whole, the unity' (*Aspects of the Novel*, p. 136), and rhythm giving the sense that a novel 'is stitched internally' (*Aspects of the Novel*, p. 146). To Forster, concepts such as 'organicism', 'unity', 'wholeness' and 'pattern' tend to define the beautiful, but we gain a further sense of what he would describe as beauty when he describes the function of rhythm: 'not to be there all the time like a pattern, but by its lovely waxing and waning to fill us with surprise and freshness and hope' (*Aspects of the Novel*, p. 148).

Forster concludes his chapter on pattern and rhythm with a description of how he would, ideally, unite the two elements of the novel, the human and the artistic. Significantly, the reconciliation is through a new kind of ending. He has previously commented on the imposition of finality on the novel, saying that the human longing for permanence leads us to accept, for example, the conventional ending of marriage, gladly, for 'we lend [novelists] our dreams' (*Aspects of the Novel*, p. 63). But the 'life' of the novel disappears with the need to create, structurally, an ending: 'nothing is heard but hammering and screwing' (*Aspects of the Novel*, p. 94). Both the humanity and the art of the novel are lost. The new kind of ending, on the other hand, would be 'Expansion. That is the idea the novelist must cling to. Not completion. Not rounding off but opening out' (*Aspects of the Novel*, p. 149). This would, it seems, unite humanity with the patterning and structure of art, and create an effect like that of great music.

Throughout *Aspects of the Novel*, Forster has stated 'History develops, Art stands still' (*Aspects of the Novel*, pp. 36, 151); the novel, being an art-form, is therefore timeless, and Forster encourages his audience to imagine all novelists writing together at the same time in a circular room. He also justifies this ahistorical approach by referring to the novel's close link with human nature. To Forster, human nature may change, but it will take considerably longer than the four hundred years that the novel as we know it has existed. This profound, and somewhat literal, humanism, allied to a celebration of art's timelessness, releases Forster from the necessity of considering social, historical or material influences on the composition and production of fiction. According to Forster, the writer's desire to write is the vital factor. *Aspects of the Novel* concentrates on the constituents of fiction, such as story, plot, characters, and pattern; Forster's humanist emphasis also enables him to discuss more technical issues, such as 'point of view', very cursorily.

In fact, the question of 'point of view' is particularly interesting, because Forster's own use of it in his fiction is idiosyncratic. In *Aspects of the Novel*, he displays the pragmatism of the practising writer in his reluctance to analyse the techniques or effects of point of view. There are two criteria by which to discuss point of view, for Forster: the 'power of the writer to bounce the reader into accepting what he says' (*Aspects of the Novel*, p. 82), and the fact that an erratic use of viewpoint reflects how human beings actually perceive life. Thus, to Forster, the writer's use of point of view is judged in terms of verisimilitude at both extremes of the contract between reader and author: point of view should reflect how we see life, and that use of point of view is effective if we are convinced by it. It is worth noting, here, that he insists on the importance of the author's power and omniscience vis-à-vis the presentation of his or her characters. Correspondingly, his own distinctive and shifting point of view in his novels is justified and explained by his comments in *Aspects of the Novel*. The power of the novelist to reveal the 'secret life' of his or her characters, and the power to play fast and loose with his or her mode of narration, are closely connected – 'All that matters to the reader is whether the shifting of attitude and the secret life are convincing' (*Aspects of the Novel*, p. 86).

So far, Forster's discussion of the novel reveals great ideological faith in the scope of the realist novel, and a great affection for its human and artistic potential. However, Forster's desire to end the novel with 'expansion' suggests an unease with some of the realist features of the novel: that confidence, for example, that the novel unproblematically reflects life and also imposes a comforting order on life's experiences. To Forster, there is a third element, that occurs in his novels, and that he discusses at length in *Aspects of the Novel*. It could be called, variously, vision, prophecy or symbolism. Forster himself has difficulty ascribing a name to it, but he says, 'There is more in the novel than time or people or logic or any of their derivatives, more even than fate' (*Aspects of the Novel*, p. 102). In discussions of Dostoyevsky and Melville, he attempts to describe an element which, while not integral to the novel as a form, is an extra dimension, giving access to mystical and profound regions. For example, Dostoyevsky's characters convey to us a sensation that is partly physical – the sensation of sinking into a translucent globe and seeing our experience floating far above us on its surface, tiny, remote, yet ours. We have not ceased to be people, we have given nothing up, but 'the sea is in the fish and the fish is in the sea'. (*Aspects of the Novel*, p. 123)

At this level, Forster rejects precision, preferring to attempt to describe a visionary extension of experience. He refuses to pin down the symbolism of *Moby Dick*, saying, 'Nothing can be stated about *Moby Dick* except that it is a contest. The rest is song' (*Aspects of the Novel*, p. 128).

There are, then, it might be said, three areas which concern Forster, to do with the novel: people, artistic demands, and visionary elements. In these concerns we may discern the constituents which, when brought together in a delicate balance, cause the tensions, difficulties and attractions of Forster's novels. Many critics identify different, competing claims for the reader's attention in Forster's novels. Lionel Trilling, for example, using the terms 'story' and 'plot' in ways that are not Forster's, suggests that the story of *A Passage to India* and the plot of *A Passage to India* are quite different, the plot being

precise, hard, crystallized and far simpler than any Forster has previously conceived. The story is beneath and above the plot and continues beyond it in time ... The characters are of sufficient size for the plot; they are not large enough for the story – and that indeed is the point of the story.

As we have already seen, John Beer claims that Forster's plots do not contain the central impetus of the novels, and therefore disappoint the unwary reader. Peter Widdowson discusses the contradiction between realism and symbolism in the ending of *Howards End*: the ending expresses both a symbolic harmony between the different characters and values in the novel, and a pessimism about the tensions of the liberal-humanist position. Malcolm Bradbury notes Forster's ' "poetic" evocation of the world of mystery, and a "comic" evocation of the world of muddle'. It is perhaps in the dialectic between 'mystery' and 'muddle', between the transcendent and quotidian worlds, that Forster's strengths and weaknesses lie. These terms recur frequently in the novels. 'Mystery' remains, always for Forster, the secret, unknowable and sacred part of the individual and, ultimately, of the universe. 'Muddle', on the other hand, is the characteristic state of the social life, and can be comic, haphazard and regarded affectionately, or can reflect the falsities imposed by social rules and selfishness. In *A Passage to India*, it seems that mystery resides within muddle: the transcendent unity of life which beckons as an ideal throughout the novel can only be perceived through the muddled and tiring process of life in India. Forster uses these characteristically woolly terms in ways that reflect his insistence on the right to change his mind. It is a right that vindicates his liberal-humanist position, but that sometimes leads to a conflict of aims and techniques.

Forster's sense of the mystery in people and in the universe indicates a deeply felt debt to Romanticism. His early novels, in particular, express a sense of place and moments of nature-worship, such as the Wiltshire landscape in *The Longest Journey*, the house and garden of *Howards End*, the woods of *Maurice*. Yet his attitude to a post-Darwinian universe is more ambivalent than that of the Romantic poets. *A Passage to India* conveys a far more disturbing sense of nature's unknowable mysteries, a sense terrifyingly manifested in the caves, which 'robbed infinity and eternity of their vastness' (p. 161).

Forster's attitude towards the mystery of people is similarly tentative. In an essay of 1920, he recorded his opinion that 'the character of the English is essentially middle-class' ('Notes on the English Character', *Abinger Harvest*, p. 13). The middle classes are characterized by 'solidity, caution, integrity, efficiency. Lack of imagination, hypocrisy.' To Forster the heart of the English middle classes is the public-school system, and this has created the English character. The public school creates men, Forster says, 'with well-developed bodies, fairly developed minds, and undeveloped hearts. And it is this undeveloped heart that is largely responsible for the difficulties of Englishmen abroad. An undeveloped heart – not a cold one' (*Abinger Harvest*, p. 15). Later in the essay Forster says:

> The main point of these notes is that the English character is incomplete. No national character is complete. We have to look for some qualities in one part of the world and others in another. But the English character is incomplete in a way that is particularly annoying to the foreign observer. It has a bad surface – self-complacent, unsympathetic, and reserved. There is plenty of emotion further down, but it never gets used. There is plenty of brain power, but it is more often used to confirm prejudices than to dispel them. With such an equipment the Englishman cannot be popular. Only I would repeat: there is little vice in him and no real coldness. It is the machinery that is wrong. (*Abinger Harvest*, p. 25)

In his novels Forster presents characters who display this philistin-ism, complacency, and inhibiting puritanism. They are always a target for his scorn, and in *A Passage to India* the dangers of such characteristics are shown up in the Anglo-Indian society, with far-reaching implications for the Imperialist endeavour. But Forster also presents characters whose 'undeveloped hearts' are worked upon and transformed to some degree. In *A Passage to India* both Adela and Fielding, in different ways, are confronted with the experience of India and with Indians like Aziz, who asks, ' "Is emotion a sack of potatoes, so much the pound, to be measured out?" ' (p. 253).

It is 'Love the Beloved Republic' that Forster gives three cheers to, and the great sin for him is the sin against affection. Yet he aims both to display the 'secret life' of his characters and to satirize the lack of feeling in some of them. It is a contradiction between poetry and comedy, mystery and muddle. As Forster says of Dostoyevsky, 'The extension, the melting, the unity through love and pity occur in a region which can only be implied, and to which fiction is perhaps the wrong approach' (*Aspects of the Novel*, p. 123).

3. The British in India

British rule in India took the form of a direct and an indirect presence, and Forster neatly illustrates this division in his novel by moving the action from the direct rule of Chandrapore to the indirect rule of Mau. What was termed British India, subject to direct rule, comprised some 60 per cent of the sub-continent, and was divided up into seven provinces, each with its own governor. The remaining 40 per cent of the Indian land-mass was the province of the Indian princes, and was composed of approximately six hundred native states of widely varying size. The population of the sub-continent at the height of British rule, between 1860 and the Great War of 1914–18, consisted of 70 per cent Hindus, 20 per cent Muslims, 3 per cent Buddhists, 3 per cent Animists and other sects, and 1 per cent Christians. The native states, while not strictly part of British India, owed allegiance to the British crown, and were controlled ultimately by the Governor-General in his role as Viceroy. There were Residents or British Agents in all the important states, but in most cases the ruler occupied a feudal throne without overt interference from the Raj. The native princes notably remained loyal to Britain during the Mutiny of 1857–9. British India was organized into a three-tier system with a Secretary of State responsible to Parliament in London. The framework of rule was sustained by the almost exclusively British Indian Civil Service, which possessed one thousand officials in 1900.

The six decades between the end of the Mutiny in the late 1850s and the end of the Great War in 1918 saw the British presence in India reach its peak. It was also, however, the period when the consciousness of nationalism was born. In 1859 the Government of India Act transferred British power from the East India Company to the crown. The Viceroy was supreme after reorganization, and there was now little pretence that imperial rule was not imperialist in intention. The Viceroy ruled essentially through the ICS (Indian Civil Service) which was manned by Englishmen who, after 1853, entered it through competitive examinations. The supremacy of the Raj was manifested in the 1876 declaration of Queen Victoria as Empress of India. Such acts, however, could not bridge the gap of racial tension left behind after the failure of the Mutiny. The British government did have a real interest in Indian welfare, but it was primarily the interest of a world power utilizing Indian raw materials and man-power. The chief concern throughout this period was the consolidation of power through greater efficiency in the Indian army and a higher degree of professionalism in the I C S. Communications were improved as part of this effort of dominance: there was a large-scale railway building programme, and the opening of the Suez Canal and introduction of steamships in 1869, and the marine telegraph cable laid in 1865, all served to bring governance of the sub-continent closer to Westminster. While the intellectual calibre of the I C S greatly increased after the introduction of competitive examinations, the sympathy and understanding of Indian life and culture necessarily diminished through the importation of personnel from England.

Nationalism in India during the late nineteenth century tended to be rather an ambivalent movement. The Indian National Congress, a focus for primarily Hindu aspirations, first met in 1885. Congress was largely an amalgamation of lawyers, businessmen, journalists and academics, and argued against the so-called economic 'drain' of India by the British. As a movement it did not attract the Muslims, who formed separate organizations of their own. Nationalist feeling was greatly exacerbated by the high-handed nature of Lord Curzon's viceroyalty (1899–1905), and the partition of Bengal in 1905 inflamed emotions still further. These feelings were countered to some extent by the British desire to bring Indians into closer connection with the administration by enlarging the powers of the existing legislative councils. At the same time efforts were made to bring the princes more fully into the governing process. In return for the loss of their purely nominal independence, the princes were made subordinate partners in the Raj. As a result of splits in the Congress movement early in the new century, two movements emerged. One, led by Gokhale, urged gradual reform; the other, led by Tilak, espoused more revolutionary aims.

The victory of the Liberal Party in the British election of 1906 enabled concessions to be made to nationalist opinion which may have headed off insurrection. Under the Minto–Morley reforms of 1909 Indians were admitted to membership of the provincial executive councils and the Imperial Legislative council was enlarged to incorporate an elected element. The viceroy still reigned supreme, but the reforms were a step towards representative government in India. The new era of cooperation between rulers and ruled was symbolically inaugurated in 1911 by the great Delhi Durbar presided over by the newly crowned George V and Queen Mary, and by the removal of the capital from Calcutta to New Delhi.

However, the 'honeymoon' between Congress and the British government was soon disrupted by the Great War, an event which produced a revolution in Indian consciousness. Initially, Congress and the princes were loyal supporters of the war effort, while the Muslim community was divided because of its allegiance to the Caliph of Turkey, who was being attacked by the British. Large numbers of Indians served on the Western Front and elsewhere, but as the war dragged on critical voices were heard. The Great War proved to the subjugated Indian population that the Raj was not invincible. Other world events, such as the Russian Revolution of 1917, and the American insistence upon independence and self-determination, unsettled the native Indian groupings on the subcontinent. Because of the war the ICS was depleted of personnel and run by an increasingly exhausted bureaucracy. The national mood of irritation and restlessness was further stirred by the disastrous flu epidemic which killed upwards of five million people in India alone. As the war dragged towards its close, in 1917, the British government felt compelled by these and other factors to announce a change of policy, a change which advocated

increasing association of Indians in every branch of the administration, and the gradual development of self-governing institutions, with a view to the progressive realization of responsible government in India as an integral part of the Empire.

This declaration paved the way for final independence, which was to come in 1947. The reforms were inaugurated in 1921, around the period of the action of the novel. The executive council was now manned by moderates, and self-government seemed to be a distant but realizable aim. But the fate of the constitution was not to be decided by lawyers and politicians. Before the new constitution came into being, Home Rule agitation and the Lucknow Pact between Muslims and Hindus registered an irrevocable split between the British and their colonial subjects. The so-called Rowlatt Bills, which had been aimed at stifling terrorism, focused indignation and paved the way for the passive resistance movement inaugurated at the end of the war by Mohandas Gandhi, a middle-aged lawyer recently returned from a campaign of passive resistance in South Africa. Gandhi proposed a campaign of *hartal* – the

31

cessation of all work for a day on a national scale. During 1919 and 1920 his non-cooperation movement spread throughout the sub-continent, but resistance focused in the Punjab. In April 1919, General Dyer ordered armed soldiers to fire on an unarmed crowd of ten thousand at Amritsar in the Punjab. As a result, four hundred people were killed and twelve hundred wounded. Dyer was retired, but was greeted as a hero by some in Britain and offered a vote of thanks by the House of Lords. Gandhi now introduced his *satyagraha* movement, which advocated a boycott of British goods, educational institutions, and employment. At this time Gandhi laboured hard to bring the Muslims into his movement, but the split with their leader Jinnah led to separatist claims which finally formed the basis for the setting up of Pakistan. Gandhi was arrested in 1922, and released in 1924, the year of the publication of *A Passage to India*. The move towards independence grew stronger in the next decade, but its impetus was delayed by the outbreak of war in 1939. Indian independence was not finally achieved until 1947, under the post-war Labour administration led by Clement Attlee.

4. Forster's Involvement with India

Forster's visits to India in 1912–13 and in 1921 provided him with the knowledge and experience of the country and the people that were to form the basis of *A Passage to India*. When the novel was published, there was some criticism, from various quarters, of his depiction of Anglo-Indians and Indians. Forster defended himself in a letter to one critic in these terms:

I have only been to the country twice (year and a half in all), and only been acquainted with Indians for eighteen years, yet I believe that I have seen certain important truths that have been hidden from you despite your thirty years' service on the spot, and despite your highly specialized training.

In fact, Forster acquired an impressive variety of experiences and acquaintances, and his years in Alexandria deepened his awareness of Islam and the Oriental temperament. His first visit to India was prompted by his friendship with Syed Ross Masood, and he went out not as an administrator, politician or journalist, but as a friend and guest. He was, therefore, able to mix with the people he met with a certain freedom from imposed roles or preconceptions. This was what he wanted, at any rate; when he returned to India in 1921, he went to act as private secretary to the Rajah of Dewas State Senior, whom he had met during his first visit. His letters often express a satisfaction that he is the only Englishman for miles around, that he has witnessed rituals 'in which a European can seldom have shared' (*The Hill of Devi*, p. 99), and that he has in a small way broken down some barriers: 'For four hours yesterday evening I walked barefoot in petticoats through the streets with black and red powders smeared over my forehead, cheeks and nose' (*The Hill of Devi*, p. 106). Forster's two visits familiarized him with India to a comparatively unusual extent, although his encounters were limited to Indians of certain social groupings. His visits also demonstrated to him practically the differences between the races and cultures. He left Dewas State Senior at the end of 1921 with a feeling of exasperation as well as of friendship, and it is with the authority of experience that he writes about Indians' ways of life, and about the muddle and mysticism of India.

During his first visit, Forster socialized with Masood and his friends, and also spent some time with Anglo-Indians. He travelled widely and saw many of the famous Indian tourist sights. He experienced a blankness in the Indian landscape which the reader finds similarly portrayed in *A Passage to India*:

Since leaving the station we had seen nothing but crops and people, and birds, and horses as feeble as our own. The track we were following wavered and blurred, and offered alternatives; it had no earnestness of purpose like the tracks of England. And the crops were haphazard too – flung this way and that on the enormous earth, with patches of brown between them. There was no place for anything, and nothing was in its place. There was no time either. All the small change of the north rang false, and nothing remained certain but the dome of the sky and the disk of the sun. ('Adrift in India', 1914, *Abinger Harvest*, p. 324)

The unreliability of Indians' invitations, the lack of differentiation between objects, the tiringness of the landscape – all these observations occurred to Forster during his first visit. But perhaps the most lasting impressions that he gained were through his meetings with two temperamentally very different men, the Maharajah of Chhatarpur and the Rajah of Dewas State Senior. They were both devout Hindus, and 'they have between them helped to illuminate Indian religion for me' (*The Hill of Devi*, p. 27). The Maharajah of Chhatarpur described his meditations to Forster:

'I try to meditate on Krishna. I do not know that he is a God, but I love Love and Beauty and Wisdom, and I find them in his history. I worship and adore him as a man. If he is divine he will notice me for it and reward me; if he is not, I shall become grass and dust like the others.' (*The Hill of Devi*, p. 26)

Forster immediately felt drawn to the Rajah of Dewas State Senior, calling him 'the beloved Rajah of Dewas' (*The Hill of Devi*, p. 23), and, of course, returned to him in 1921. Both men shared similarities with Forster's character Professor Godbole, and their respective princely states both recur in Forster's description of Mau. Another, relatively brief, meeting provided Forster with some aspects of Aziz's character. Abu Saeed Mirza, the brother of one of Masood's friends, entertained Forster towards the end of his visit. He was impulsive and volatile, and one day, when riding with Forster, told him, ' "It may be fifty or five hundred years but we shall turn you out" '.

Although Forster's interest in India centred upon the life, culture and variety of the land, he was inevitably engaged by the political currents. His first visit revealed the Anglo-Indians to him as being intolerant and unsympathetic, on the whole, and he left India on this occasion with a 'sense of racial tension, of incompatibility'. The contradictions between tradition and innovation within the Indian way of life disturbed him when he attended a wedding between Muslims conducted along rationalist lines:

It was depressing, almost heartrending, and opened the problem of India's future. How could this jumble end? Before the Moulvi finished a gramophone began, and before that was silent a memorable act took place. The sun was setting, and the orthodox withdrew from us to perform their evening prayer. They gathered on the terrace behind, to the number of twenty, and prostrated themselves towards Mecca. Here was dignity and unity; here was a great tradition untainted by private judgement; they had not retained so much and rejected so much; they had accepted Islam unquestioningly, and the reward of such an acceptance is beauty ... Crash into the devotions of the orthodox birred the gramophone –

I'd sooner be busy with my little Lizzie,

and by a diabolic chance reached the end of its song as they ended the prayer. They rejoined us without self-consciousness, but the sun and the snows were theirs, not ours; they had obeyed; we had entered the unlovely chaos that lies between obedience and freedom   and that seems, alas! the immediate future of India. ('Adrift in India', 1914, *Abinger Harvest*, pp. 329–30)

But Forster's concern for the future of India never embraced the plight of the millions of poor, underfed peasants, nor did it develop into political activity. When he returned to India in 1921, the tensions between the British and the Indians were far greater, but he succeeded in creating an experience of friendship and intimacy that seems far away from the mood of Gandhi's growing non-cooperation movement. The Rajah of Dewas State Senior inevitably supported the British rather than Gandhi, as Forster explains in 'The Mind of the Indian Native State' (1922, *Abinger Harvest*, pp. 352–64), and Forster found himself writing, from Dewas:

It will be curious to see something of the India that is changing. There is no perceptible change here, indeed the atmosphere is in some ways less western than it was nine years ago. No one, except myself, wears European clothes, for instance – nine years ago H.H. often did. The place is altogether exceptional, and generalizations from it, which I am sure to make, are sure to be wrong. There is no anti-English feeling. It is Gandhi whom they dread and hate. (*The Hill of Devi*, p. 89)

In 1923, Forster expounds his liberal-humanist views on this matter; he is talking about the Middle East rather than India, but his recent experiences provide a useful context: 'we who seek the truth are only concerned with politics when they deflect us from it. The individual in the East must succeed as an individual or he has failed' ('Salute to the Orient!', *Abinger Harvest*, p. 288).

During his second visit Forster once again spent some time with Masood, but on the whole experienced at first hand many aspects of the day-to-day life of a small royal court. Temporarily replacing the Secretary who was on home leave, he found that he was expected to organize practical matters such as the electricity generator, the watering of the garden, and car maintenance, but also found that his company and attendance were deemed sufficient and appreciated. He frequently dressed in Indian clothes, as he had with the Rajah during his first visit; the comment in *A Passage to India* is from personal experience:

Fielding, who had dressed up in a native costume, learned from his excessive awkwardness in it that all his motions were makeshifts, whereas when the Nawab Bahadur stretched out his hand for food, or Nureddin applauded a song, something beautiful had been accomplished which needed no development. This restfulness of gesture – it is the Peace that passeth Understanding, after all, it is the social equivalent of Yoga. When the whirring of action ceases, it becomes visible, and reveals a civilization which the West can disturb but will never acquire. The hand stretches out for ever, the lifted knee has the eternity though not the sadness of the grave. (pp. 250–51)

Forster was able to witness, and even participate in, the numerous religious occasions, which culminated in Gokul Ashtami (the birth of Krishna), the festival portrayed so prominently in the third section of *A Passage to India*. He came to understand the nuances of protocol that dictated relations among the native princes, and between them and the British, at one point even being 'Insulted' by a British official. He attempted to start a literary society, but found the cultural barriers too great; the only Western literature that he found could grasp the genuine attention of his Indian hosts was a Russian tale. Above all, though, he was exasperated, amused and attracted by the muddle of Indian life and of the Rajah: the waste of decaying pianos languishing in the palace, the inadequate supplies of water to the expensively laid out gardens, the presence of squirrels and fawns in the palace rooms. Forster finally left in a mood of despondency:

I hated leaving him, but it is his tragedy not to know how to employ people, and I could not feel it any use to go on muddling with work that gave me no satisfaction, and was of no essential importance to him. The things of this life mean so little to him – mean something so different, anyway – I never feel certain what he likes, or even whether he likes me; consideration for others so often simulates affection in him. (*The Hill of Devi*, p. 152)

It is *The Hill of Devi*, published in 1953, which provides much of the information about Forster's two visits to India. The book comprises an edited version of some of his letters home, with interlinking comments provided by Forster, and it is designed to be a study of, and tribute to, the Rajah of Dewas State Senior. It is equally interesting as a source-book for some of the events in *A Passage to India*: the accident to the Nawab's car and the mistaken identification of a tree-stump as a snake are two examples. Forster's series of letters about Gokul Ashtami forms the basis of his description of the festival in many details. In addition, the book conveys Forster's range of reactions to India with great immediacy, and demonstrates how his visit to Dewas was 'the great opportunity of my life' (*The Hill of Devi*, p. 10). He had travelled to India partly to escape the inhibitions and restrictions of his life in England, and found that he shared a sense of affinity with many Indians. India became, paradoxically, the place where he enjoyed friendship and acceptance, but also a paradigm to him of the difficulties of forging relationships. By the end of his visit, despite his own success in living with Indians, he wrote,

English manners out here have improved wonderfully in the last eight years. Some people are frightened, others seem really to have undergone a change of heart. But it's too late. Indians don't long for social intercourse with Englishmen any longer. They have made a life of their own. (*The Hill of Devi*, p. 153)

Forster made one more visit to India: to attend the Indian PEN Conference in 1945. His reactions on that occasion are described in 'India Again' (*Two Cheers for Democracy*, pp. 323–32). *A Passage to India* brought him many Indian friends over the years, and he consistently supported Indian writers by helping them to achieve publication.

5. The Composition of the Novel

I began this novel before my 1921 visit, and took out the opening chapters with me, with the intention of continuing them. But as soon as they were confronted with the country they purported to describe, they seemed to wilt and go dead and I could do nothing with them. I used to look at them of an evening in my room at Dewas, and felt only distaste and despair. The gap between India remembered and India experienced was too wide. When I got back to England the gap narrowed, and I was able to resume. But I still thought the book bad, and probably should not have completed it without the encouragement of Leonard Woolf. (*The Hill of Devi*, pp. 153–4)

The development of *A Passage to India* was lengthy and difficult. On his first visit to India, Forster saw many of the places he was to utilize, for example, Bankipore (Chandrapore), the Barabar Caves (the Marabar), Chhatarpur and Dewas State Senior (Mau). The central character of Aziz was already known to him, based on some of the traits of Abu Saeed Mirza, and more generally on Syed Ross Masood. Forster grew to love Masood, finally dedicating the novel to him:

He woke me up out of my suburban and academic life, showed me new horizons and a new civilization and helped me towards the understanding of a continent. Until I met him, India was a vague jumble... ('Syed Ross Masood', 1937, *Two Cheers for Democracy*, p. 296)

On his return to England in the early summer of 1913, Forster began work on an Indian novel, but soon dropped it in favour of his secret homosexual novel, *Maurice*. He said later that he was clear about the 'chief characters and the racial tension, had visualized the scenery and had foreseen that something 'crucial would happen in the Marabar Caves. But I had not seen far enough.' During the war, in Alexandria, Forster inevitably let the novel drop, and only felt able to return to his manuscript after his return from India in 1922. Through the valued advice of Leonard Woolf, who had himself worked as a colonial administrator, Forster was able to complete the work, though it was apparently cast in a more pessimistic tone than that first envisaged. He still worked slowly, complaining that he felt that 'the characters are not sufficiently interesting for the atmosphere'. By early 1924, however, he was working on the final chapters, excited and uplifted by his reading of T. E. Lawrence's *Seven Pillars of Wisdom*, which dealt with the Arab revolt.

The novel had taken more than a decade to write and reflects impressions gained from visits undertaken in very different political circumstances. Forster dealt with this problem by making it a novel 'out of time', without specific reference to dates or events, although several critics have detected anachronisms, particularly in the depiction of Anglo-Indian society. In the final stages of composition, Forster decided to name the book after the title of a poem by the American, Walt Whitman:

the book is not really about politics, though it is the political aspect of it that caught the general public and made it sell. It's about something wider than politics, about the search of the human race for a more lasting home, about the universe as embodied in the Indian earth and the horror lurking in the Marabar Caves and the release symbolized by the birth of Krishna. It is – or rather desires to be – philosophic and poetic, and that is why when I had finished it I took its title, 'Passage to India', from a famous poem of Walt Whitman's.*

The novel was published by Edward Arnold in June 1924.

* 'Three Countries', an unpublished manuscript quoted by John Colmer, *E. M. Forster: The Personal Voice* (Routledge and Kegan Paul, 1975), p. 156.

6. The Title of the Novel and a Synopsis

Forster derived the title of his novel from a poem by the American poet, Walt Whitman (1819–92). Whitman was an ardently democratic poet who hymned the formation of the American nation. His poetry, in its rhythmic and stanzaic energy and freedom, mirrors his free-wheeling expansionist philosophy of life, a philosophy summed up in his words, 'I am large, I contain multitudes'. The metaphor of the mystical journey dominates Whitman's poetry and language, and his works enjoyed a great vogue in the early years of this century, being set to music by Delius, Vaughan Williams, Holst and others.

'A Passage to India', written in 1871, is one of Whitman's most eloquent works. It poses a question asked by the 'feverish children' of the modern age, 'Whither, O mocking life?', and begins by celebrating the marriage of the seas through the opening up of the Suez canal:

> *Passage to India!*
> *Lo, soul, seest thou not God's purpose from the first?*
> *The earth to be spann'd, connected by network,*
> *The races, neighbors, to marry and be given in marriage,*
> *The oceans to be cross'd, the distant brought near,*
> *The lands to be welded together.*

> *A worship new I sing,*
> *You captains, voyagers, explorers, yours,*
> *You engineers, you architects, machinists, yours,*
> *You, not for trade or transportation only,*
> *But in God's name, and for thy sake, O soul.*

Perhaps hinting at the Forsterian theme of connection between peoples, Whitman rejoices at the 'lands to be welded together' through engineering and exploration. Superseding the mechanical men, however, is the poet, who Whitman believes will 'fuse' all lands and people through his vision. The poem culminates in a pantheistic triumph which Forster's more muted tone refuses. The soul seeks passage to 'more than India':

Sail forth – steer for the deep water only,
Reckless O soul, exploring, I with thee, and thou with me,
For we are bound where mariner has not yet dared to go,
And we will risk the ship, ourselves and all.

Synopsis of the novel

The reader is introduced to the Indian town of Chandrapore. It is a mixture of old and new, and apart from the nearby Marabar Caves possesses no unusual features. The older Indian section of town is a maze of streets and bazaars, while the British civil station on the hill is tidily laid out with modern buildings. Aziz, a Muslim doctor, works here. He and his circle of friends, which includes Hamidullah, a barrister, and Mahmoud Ali, a lawyer, discuss among themselves relations with the ruling British. Aziz is sent for by his superior, Major Callendar, but on arrival finds that the colonel has gone out. Returning to the native quarter, Aziz enters a mosque and encounters an elderly English woman, Mrs Moore. He feels an instinctive liking for her and they have a lively conversation. Mrs Moore is the mother of the City Magistrate, Ronny Heaslop. She has come to India accompanied by a young girl, Adela Quested, who is considering marriage to Ronny.

Mrs Moore and Adela wish to see the true India, and Mr Turton, the Collector, arranges a 'Bridge Party' to allow them to meet representative Indians. The party is a failure since neither side goes beyond polite civilities. The women meet Cyril Fielding at the party, and recognize in him a civilized and liberal friend of the Indian community. He invites them both to tea at his house in the local government college, of which he is Principal. Here they meet Aziz, and the Hindu Professor Godbole. Aziz is loquacious and tells of the Mogul emperors whom he admires. He invites the party to join him in an expedition to the Marabar Caves, a natural feature whose significance Godbole refuses to disclose. Ronny Heaslop arrives and angrily takes the women away, as Godbole sings an ancient Hindu song.

The friendship between Aziz and Fielding develops rapidly. Fielding pays Aziz a visit, and the Muslim shows his friend a photograph of his dead wife. Fielding says that he himself will never marry, and confesses to Aziz that he is an agnostic. He finds Adela rather a prig, and extols the values of freedom, and personal relationships.

The Marabar Caves are described in detail. They are situated in north-east India, in the Marabar Hills. Inside them nothing is to be found. Aziz makes elaborate preparations for his expedition. Mrs Moore and Adela arrive promptly to catch the train, but Fielding and Godbole are delayed and miss it. When the party arrives at the Hills, they enter a cave. Mrs Moore is struck by something, and undergoes a spiritual crisis. She comes out having lost all interest in life; everything is reduced to nothingness by the echo effect in the cave. Aziz and Adela move to another cave, and as they enter Adela asks him how many wives he has. Aziz, pained by this question, loses sight of Adela and assumes she is in another cave. When he emerges from his own cave he finds she has vanished, leaving behind her broken field-glasses. Returning down the hill, he is pleased to meet Fielding. Adela has run down the hill in a panic, getting badly pricked by cactuses in the process. She then returns to town with her friend Miss Derek.

When the rest of the party returns to Chandrapore railway station, Aziz is immediately arrested. Fielding is shocked. Aziz is accused of trying to molest Adela in the cave. The atmosphere in Chandrapore becomes tense and panicky. The prospect of Aziz's trial polarizes the Indian and British communities, but serves to unite Muslim and Hindu. A distinguished nationalistic lawyer, Mr Amritrao, is engaged to defend Aziz. Fielding sides with Aziz, and resigns from the Club. Adela complains of hearing an echo in her head. Mrs Moore is listless and uninterested, and decides to return to England before the trial. Fielding holds a baffling interview with Godbole about what may have occurred in the caves.

At the trial of Aziz, Mr McBryde presents the case for the prosecution. He gives an outline of Adela's story, but when he questions her about Aziz following her into the cave, she replies that she is unsure. The prosecution case is destroyed and Aziz is declared not guilty. Adela is renounced by her own side, but her echo is now silenced. Fielding is forced reluctantly to accommodate her at his house, but goes on to join Aziz in his victory celebrations. The news comes through that Mrs Moore has died while en route to England. Aziz is pained by this news, and is persuaded not to press Adela for damages. She will no longer marry Ronny, and leaves for England, intending to look up Ralph and Stella, Mrs Moore's children by her second marriage.

The scene shifts to the native state of Mau. Two years have passed. Godbole is Minister of Education here, and Aziz is personal physician to the Maharajah. Fielding, after a visit to England, is now an inspector of schools. Godbole dances on a carpet before images of the god. It is the festival of Gokul Ashtami, celebrating the birth of Krishna. The people are seized with mirth and high spirits. Godbole, in a trance-like state, invokes the memory of Mrs Moore, and sings a song about Tukaram, an Indian saint. Later, he informs Aziz of the arrival of Fielding and others at the state's Guest House. Fielding is to inspect the state schools, and is accompanied by his wife and her brother. Aziz suspects that Fielding must have married Adela and that he has consequently been robbed of his compensation money. Fielding wishes to watch the torchlight procession near the Mau lake.

Aziz takes his children for a walk in the monsoon, and they visit a shrine. The Maharajah is dead, but the news is not to be released until the festivities are at an end. Aziz meets Fielding and Ralph Moore. They talk, but the conversation is not cordial. Aziz now learns that Fielding has in fact married Stella, Mrs Moore's daughter. Later Aziz visits the Guest House with medicine for Ralph, who has been stung by bees. He likes the youth, and learns from him that Fielding and Stella have gone out boating on the lake. Aziz and Ralph join them as they try to watch the climax of the festivities on the banks. The boats collide, and they fall into the shallow water.

Later, Aziz and Fielding go on a final horse-ride together. Fielding wants their friendship to be renewed. Aziz replies that they can never be true friends until India is free. Only on the basis of political equality is true friendship between individuals possible. Fielding presses his ideal of friendship, but the environment replies, 'No, not yet'.

7. Commentary and Analysis

Themes and characterization

It is appropriate to begin a discussion of the themes of *A Passage to India* with the ways in which India is portrayed and discussed in the novel. India is at once the vast continent, situated geographically, historically and climatically for the characters and the reader, and a symbol of the passage of every human spirit to a new environment, culture and dimension, challenging the individual to respond in the ways he or she best can. 'India' assumes a nebulous character of its own in the novel: the questions are frequently posed as to what India is, or means, and whether it exists except as a term that cannot encompass its variety. In one sense, India is all-inclusive, being the Marabar Caves and the coconut palms that bid farewell to Mrs Moore, the Anglo-Indians, Muslims, Hindus, missionaries and untouchables, the hot season and the rainy season. India is also eternally divided and divisive, historically subject to the colonial ambitions of other races and, in its climate and terrain, inhospitable to the aspirations of human beings.

The main English characters all make their 'passage to India' in the novel. Adela wishes to see the 'real' India, but she is never really sure what she is looking for: whether it is the people, the scenery, the customs, or the history. She wishes to understand, but her attempts to understand always lead to offence rather than friendship, for, as Forster makes clear, her desire is 'theoretical' rather than heart-felt. Ronny is sure he has found the 'real' India through his handful of second-hand opinions and phrases; content with that, his final comment in the novel consigns him to the cliché-ridden world forever: ' "My personal opinion is, it's the Jews" ' (p. 303). Mrs Moore succeeds in seeing the 'real' India where Adela fails, when she wanders into a mosque and meets Aziz for the first time, but she encounters a nihilism in the Marabar Caves that she mistakes for the whole of India. Fielding underestimates the difficulties of the country, of being easy with Indians, and his own limitations; being a rationalist, he tries to convert India into Italy, where 'The Mediterranean is the human norm' (p. 278), and to ignore the very difference of India.

The experience of India is physical as well as emotional and spiritual. The terrain is harsh and uncompromising; 'walking fatigued [Aziz], as it fatigues everyone in India except the newcomer. There is something hostile in that soil' (p. 40). The climate frays tempers, and people must stay apart, indoors, in the hot season to preserve their individuality. It affects Indians and foreigners alike, for 'in the tropics ... the inarticulate world is closer at hand and readier to resume control as soon as men are tired' (p. 126), and Forster tells us, 'the spirit of the Indian earth ... tries to keep men in compartments' (p. 141). The Marabar Hills stick up out of the earth just as, at the end of the novel, the earth sends up 'rocks through which riders must pass single-file' (p. 316). Yet from a distance, and in certain lights, the country appears beautiful and intangible. The night sky unites moon, stars and earth, giving Mrs Moore a momentary sense of unity.

Even the history of India is a series of conflicts and conquests between different races and religions. Aziz refers to the great Mogul emperors; Anglo-Indians have their own Indian history, and refer several times to the Mutiny of 1857; the native states exist alongside the British presence. There is no such thing as a historically united India; this exists only in a future. But one of the final questions that Fielding asks Aziz is how that can be achieved, even if the British agree to go. For Forster portrays the internal schisms as carefully as he does the imposition of British rule. At several points in the novel he shows the distrust and antagonism existing between Muslim and Hindu, who only unite in a common dislike of the British. The Muslim festival of Mohurram regularly produces riots; Aziz, later, is unsure how much of the Hindu festival, Gokul Ashtami, he is supposed not to witness. And towards the end of the novel, Forster adds, 'The fissures in the Indian soil are infinite: Hinduism, so solid from a distance, is riven into sects and clans' (p. 289).

It is not only the nature of 'India' that is interrogated in the novel. The character of the Indian is also discussed. The Anglo-Indians tend to cherish a series of received opinions about the other race that ignore the variety of Indians and surreptitiously uphold British superiority. They invoke their length of service in India to lend authority to these opinions; the irony is that it is Ronny who parades them, in an unconscious parody of his superiors. While Forster is keen to indicate, through his characterization and in his authorial statements, that any generalization is inaccurate, it is worth investigating these prejudices, for they form an ideological underpinning against which Forster directs much of his plot and commentary. The Anglo-Indians in *A Passage to India* stress the irresponsibility and volatility of Indians, thereby justifying the need for British rule. As Allen Greenberger has shown, in *The British Image of India*, this ideological taxonomy was general amongst British administrators in India, and Forster appears, partly, to subscribe to it when he says of Aziz, 'His face grew very tender – the tenderness of one incapable of administration, and unable to grasp that if the poor criminal is let off he will again rob the poor widow' (pp. 87–8). Yet Forster also values this tenderness and childlikeness, and there is a sadness implied when Aziz says later, ' "I was a child when you knew me first. Everyone was my friend then" ' (p. 273). Another prejudice on the part of the Anglo-Indians is a fear of Indian sensuality and a simultaneous, lascivious, preoccupation with polygamy and purdah. When Aziz is arrested and the photograph of his wife is snatched, McBryde's 'face became inquisitive and slightly bestial. "Wife indeed, I know those wives!" he was thinking' (p. 180). The central accusation, that Aziz has physically assaulted Adela in a cave, serves to confirm the colour and race prejudices of the Anglo-Indians. McBryde, once again, at the trial, rehearses the prejudice 'that the darker races are physically attracted by the fairer, but not vice versa – not a matter for bitterness this, not a matter for abuse, but just a fact which any scientific observer will confirm' (p. 222). The ironies here are manifold. An Indian points out that Adela is far less attractive than Aziz, a fact that Adela herself has privately noted; Forster has previously stressed that Indian men cannot reconcile the comparative openness of Western behaviour with femininity, and that it is the English women whom Indians mainly dislike. Likewise, the notion that the climate causes flaws in the *Indian* character that cannot be denied is ironically undercut by the fact that McBryde himself was born at Karachi, and is exposed as an adulterer later in the novel. The theories conceal convictions of superiority and possession: it is Ronny, not Adela, who is the focus of sympathy, for 'he was the recipient of all the evil intended against them by the country they had tried to serve; he was bearing the sahib's cross' (p. 192) – his status has been attacked through the assault on *his* property, Adela.

Those English with more advanced notions also harbour a simplistic view of the nature of the Indian. Yet in the absence of cliché and jingoism, Forster is more ambivalent. He shows how

Adela mistakenly imagines that Aziz is a representative Indian, and how Fielding attempts to treat Indians as Italians, yet he also conveys the virtue of their determination to communicate with Indians.

Forster's efforts go both towards indicating the difference of the Indian character because of race, culture and historical circumstance, and towards an affirmation of the shared humanity of Fielding, Aziz and Mrs Moore, in spite of those differences. In this sense, the novel poses the question, as Arnold Kettle says, of 'whether or not it is possible to be friends with an Englishman'. The answer would appear to be that relationships between Anglo-Indians and Indians cannot succeed when differences are wilfully denied. Aziz's biggest mistake is to relax at the picnic at the caves and say, ' "This picnic is nothing to do with English or Indians; it is an expedition of friends" ' (p. 170). The scenes in which Aziz and Mrs Moore first meet, and Aziz and Fielding first meet, demonstrate the gulfs and unequal relationships of power *despite* which individuals have to attempt to communicate. In the mosque, Aziz is at first peremptory with Mrs Moore and subsequently complains of his treatment at the hands of the Anglo-Indians. Mrs Moore later sees that this could be interpreted unfavourably, but she is able to see beyond the tensions: 'how false as a summary of the man; the essential life of him had been slain' (p. 55). At their first meeting, Fielding offends Aziz by saying condescendingly, ' "Post-Impressionism, indeed!" ' (p. 84), but essential good will on both sides helps to smooth things over. However, Forster preserves a basic faith in the power of love and humanist values to overcome the barriers – at times – when he makes comments such as:

These two had strange and beautiful effects on him   they were his friends, his for ever, and he theirs for ever; ... He loved them even better than the Hamidullahs, because he had surmounted obstacles to meet them, and this stimulates a generous mind. Their images remained somewhere in his soul up to his dying day, permanent additions. (p. 154)

Hospitality is a strong theme in the novel and here, again, the central catastrophe at the Marabar Caves is apt because it shows the relationships between host and guest, superior and inferior, as being diametrically opposed. The social virtues of hospitality are a part of the essential generosity of the Indian character, as Forster sees it, and they also realign the relationships between those who have entered a country and those who are born to it and in it. The novel opens tellingly with Hamidullah entertaining his friends, and Callendar's peremptory summoning of Aziz betrays his ignorance of Indians' social lives. The same evening, Aziz is able to converse with Mrs Moore in his mosque, he the host and she the visitor. Of the party at the Marabar Caves, Forster says, 'an obscure young man had been allowed to show courtesy to visitors from another country, which is what all Indians long to do' (p. 154). But while Aziz attempts to entertain the English ladies, his anxiety and insecurity prevent him from controlling events as they should be controlled. It is a scene full of pathos, from the information that Aziz is so anxious that he camps out on the station overnight to the description of the looting of all his careful provisions for the picnic after his arrest. And if it is impossible for an Indian to play host to the British in his own country, it is also difficult, it seems, for the British to wield anything but the superiority of officialdom. The Bridge Party is unsatisfactory largely because of the Anglo-Indians' cynicism and intolerance. Ronny ignores Aziz and Godbole at Fielding's tea-party because 'the only link he could be conscious of with an Indian was the official, and neither happened to be his subordinate. As private individuals he forgot them' (p. 93).

This theme of hospitality is part of a wider and more general theme in the novel of the virtues of giving and receiving. Sitting in Fielding's exquisite audience-hall in which, as Forster says, 'there was no doubt to whom the room really belonged' (p. 87), Aziz develops his ideas on the virtues of giving: ' "God would give me more when he saw I gave. Always be giving, like the Nawab Bahadur ... So we would sit giving for ever" ' (p. 87). On the other hand, one of the condemnations of the Anglo-Indians in the novel, which derives from Forster's analysis of the English character, is that they cannot give at all. Turton's invocation of his twenty-five years of service 'seemed to fill the waiting-room with their staleness and ungenerosity' (p. 173). Neither have they given their affection to Adela: after her experience, they momentarily ask themselves, 'why had they not all been kinder to the stranger, more patient, given her not only hospitality but their hearts?' (p. 187). Ultimately, for Forster, giving and receiving become one and the same, in the interchange of love and affection. But the impulse to generosity does, Forster suggests, prevent effective administration and justice, hence the debate between Ronny and Mrs Moore on how the British should rule India, Mrs Moore averring, ' "The English *are* out here to be pleasant ... Because India is part of the earth. And God has put us on the earth in order to be pleasant to each other. God ... is ... love"' (p. 70). Forster never decides how far 'love' would solve the problems of the Empire, but once again there is an implicit sadness in Aziz's permanent change after Adela's accusation. His difficulty in forgiving her and his reluctance to drop his claims for damages only give way to a longer-lasting distrust of the British. His hospitality to Ralph Moore two years later is considerably more tentative and less spontaneous than his feelings towards Mrs Moore were. Yet he is once again rewarded, this time by Ralph's espial of the image of the Rajah's father across the lake, which is visible only from one spot. 'Hastily he pulled away, feeling that his companion was not so much a visitor as a guide' (p. 308) – briefly the roles of host and guest, visitor and native, have dispersed and the barriers have disappeared.

During the Hindu festivities by the lake, images of God are thrown into the lake, 'emblems of passage; a passage not easy, not now, not here, not to be apprehended except when it is unattainable: the God to be thrown was an emblem of that' (p. 309). In this echo of the title, and of the final words of the novel, it is clear that the novel is partly about the passage towards the inevitably unattainable. Just as the novel is about the possibilities of friendship, so it also contains a call to God, a prayer for understanding and enlightenment. This difficult and mystical aspect of the novel is emphasized through Godbole's song at Fielding's tea-party:

'I say to Shri Krishna: "Come! Come to me only." The God refuses to come. I grow humble and say: "Do not come to me only. Multiply yourself into a hundred Krishnas, and let one go to each of my hundred companions, but one, O Lord of the Universe, come to me." He refuses to come.' (p. 96)

In the festival in which Godbole participates in the final section of the novel, the God does come, amid unity and disorder, but only briefly. 'Infinite Love took upon itself the form of SHRI KRISHNA, and saved the world' (p. 285). The yearning for God and Love seems, to Forster, to confer spiritual wisdom and love on the individual, but always there is emptiness in the refusal of the God to come. It is a yearning reflected in the refusal of the landscape to accord significance to the human, and also reflected in the longing for a 'Friend who never comes yet is not entirely disproved' (p. 119), for, as Aziz says, ' "The Friend: a Persian expression for God" ' (p. 273). India itself seems to be the epitome of the defeat of human aspiration:

[India] knows of the whole world's trouble, to its uttermost depth. She calls 'Come' through her hundred mouths, through objects ridiculous and august. But come to what? She has never defined. She is not a promise, only an appeal. (p. 149)

This mystical dimension to the book is used in a minor way to parody Ronny and his insensitivity. In a moment of impatience he has replied to his mother,' "India likes gods" ' (p. 69), and later in the novel the Indians mock his tendency to behave and regard himself in a god-like manner. This is a part of the patterned echoing of the novel. Ronny calls for his servant, ironically named Krishna, and 'Krishna the earth, Krishna the stars replied, until the Englishman was appeased by their echoes' (p. 111). Later, when he calls to see Adela at Fielding's house after the débâcle of the trial, Hamidullah says mockingly of his arrival, ' "He comes, he comes, he comes. I cringe. I tremble" ' (p. 246).

But the major importance of the theme is the longing and striving for unifying love on both a spiritual and a human level. It is the religious impulse in its most general form. Forster may include Mohammedanism, Christianity and Hinduism in his novel, but he tends to identify them all with forms of nationalism and disunity. The religious impulse, on the other hand, is shared across religions. Mrs Moore, Godbole, Aziz, and Ralph and Stella Moore all share a reverence for the divine, which in its inclusiveness and unity appears finally to be located in some aspects of Hinduism. Any reverence for life and spirit, though, eventually comes to be regarded positively. Mrs Moore believes in ghosts, the Nawab in superstition. Their eccentricity is warmer than the rationalism and intellectualism of Fielding and Adela, who both believe in the brotherhood of man, but, respectively, disregard transcendent matters and lack essential love and compassion for other human beings. Fielding believes in 'travelling light' and places his faith in the education of the individual. He is forced to recognize that, in India at any rate, the human dimension is too small, too insignificant:

After forty years' experience, he had learned to manage his life and make the best of it on advanced European lines, had developed his personality, explored his limitations, controlled his passions – and he had done it all without becoming either pedantic or worldly. A creditable achievement, but as the moment passed he felt he ought to have been working at something else the whole time – he didn't know at what, never would know, never could know, and that was why he felt sad. (p. 197)

Adela has placed her faith in personal relations, but her mistake is less in failing to recognize a further spiritual dimension than in failing to bring her whole heart to the endeavour. Forster tells us, 'Truth is not truth in that exacting land unless there go with it kindness and more kindness and kindness again' (p. 245). Fielding and Adela sense their limitations and both return to England, accepting that the attempt to come to terms with India has required more than their philosophies and temperaments have been able to offer.

Mrs Moore's experience in the caves, and her subsequent loss of faith, puzzle many readers who cannot reconcile the positive gifts of friendship and religious impulse that she has as a character with the disillusionment and apathy that she retreats from India with. Another theme in the novel may be said to be a discussion on the effectiveness of the human scale and proportion – the liberal-humanist dilemma writ large. Mrs Moore certainly retreats from the caves with a conviction of 'Something snub-nosed, incapable of generosity – the undying worm itself' (p. 212), and her experience reduces her to feebleness and leads, eventually, to her death. Earlier in the novel, her faith in Love and God has caused her to regard a wasp on her coat-peg with affection; she has been able to include all creatures in her love. But in the caves she is faced with the insignificance of human values. Godbole, on the other hand, also tries to include all matter, all aspects of the universe, but his is an endeavour which recognizes the lack of human importance and accepts it. Both approaches see beyond the world of precedence and hierarchy which is gently satirized by Forster when he describes the missionaries struggling to include the monkeys and jackals in a Christian universe but drawing the line at bacteria. The comment, 'We must exclude someone from our gathering, or we shall be left with nothing' (p. 58), is opposed in the text by the description of the Hindu festivities, 'All spirit as well as all matter must participate in salvation, and if practical jokes are banned the circle is incomplete' (p. 286). The question is posed, in Mrs Moore's experience and in Godbole's faith, whether the human being should be accorded more value than such an all-embracing mysticism would seem to allow. Godbole's trance and ecstasy are only momentary. Both Mrs Moore and Godbole are conspicuously absent from Aziz's trial, and their apathy and disregard for legal and social life may be a criticism of such superficial processes, but are also a failing in the human dimension. When asked his opinion of what happened in the caves, Godbole replies:

'All perform a good action, when one is performed, and when an evil action is performed, all perform it. To illustrate my meaning, let me take the case in point as an example. I am informed that an evil action was performed in the Marabar Hills, and that a highly esteemed English lady is now seriously ill in consequence. My answer to that is this: that action was performed by Dr Aziz.' He stopped and sucked in his thin cheeks. 'It was performed by the guide.' He stopped again. 'It was performed by you.' Now he had an air of daring and of coyness. 'It was performed by me.' He looked shyly down the sleeve of his own coat. 'And by my students. It was even performed by the lady herself. When evil occurs, it expresses the whole of the universe. Similarly when good occurs.' (pp. 185–6)

The exposition on good and evil here does little to help Fielding in his dilemma or Aziz in his prison-cell. Godbole's slow and almost mischievous manner is presented comically by Forster, as if to underline the pointlessness of Godbole's analysis. Yet Godbole's disquisition emphasizes the communal nature of life and human beings' moral responsibility to one another. Forster certainly lends his authority to this in one sense, for after the Marabar Caves he alludes to the pervasiveness of evil several times. For example, after the trial, 'The earth and sky were insanely ugly, the spirit of evil again strode abroad' (p. 237). In a similar way, goodness is spread and shared during the Hindu festival. And while Mrs Moore as a 'person' becomes irritable and unhelpful, her spirit, or her name, becomes a benevolent influence after her death. Her name is chanted in court, she is briefly and rather ludicrously transformed into a minor Hindu goddess and she is later invoked when Aziz meets her children at Mau.

Throughout the novel there is a series of contrasts, often conveyed through the presentation of the earth and the sky, and the Indian seasons: contrasts between the finite and the infinite, the physical and the spiritual, between separation and unity, reality and illusion. The contrasts are never resolved, but form a thematic background to much that occurs to the characters in the novel. Human beings have to survive between the vast expanses of sky and earth, and frequently, it appears, the sky and the earth are at odds, especially in the hot season, trapping life in a state of alienation: 'The sky dominated as usual, but seemed unhealthily near, adhering like a ceiling to the summits of the precipices' (p. 153). Much of the novel emphasizes the physical presence of the earth, which throws up rocks, dust, and mud, and which ties human aspiration down to the mundane, for 'The very wood seems made of mud, the inhabitants of mud moving. So abased, so monotonous is everything that meets the eye, that when the Ganges comes down it might be expected to wash the excrescence back into the soil' (p. 31). In contrast, the sky, the moon and the stars seem unattainable. They confer, at night, an illusion of the spiritual – and especially towards the beginning of the novel, set during the cool season, the significant moments occur at dusk or after nightfall – but they also betray the distance between human beings and their aspirations. In fact, earth and sky seem to move closer together in the pitiless sun and to draw far apart in darkness. Although this texture in the novel is in no way schematic, it is also possible to observe that water, coming from the sky as rain and fertilizing the earth, is a unifying element which Forster uses, especially in the third section of the novel: it is set in the rainy season and its climax is when the English party and Aziz capsize their boats into the lake.

Despite, then, a tension between earth and sky portrayed in the novel, there is a possibility of harmony and unity within the universe. Mrs Moore and Aziz both experience such visions. Leaving the Club, Mrs Moore

watched the moon, whose radiance stained with primrose the purple of the surrounding sky. In England the moon had seemed dead and alien; here she was caught in the shawl of night together with earth and all the other stars. A sudden sense of unity, of kinship with the heavenly bodies, passed into the old woman and out, like water through a tank, leaving a strange freshness behind. (pp. 50–51)

Here the night sky, significantly associated with the metaphor of water, bestows a feeling of wholeness. In a similar way, Aziz, after Fielding has left his home, experiences an access of happiness:

affection had triumphed for once in a way. He dropped off to sleep amid the happier memories of the last two hours – poetry of Ghalib, female grace, good old Hamidullah, good Fielding, his honoured wife and dear boys. He passed into a region where these joys had no enemies but bloomed harmoniously in an eternal garden, or ran down watershoots of ribbed marble, or rose into domes whereunder were inscribed, black against white, the ninety-nine attributes of God. (p. 133)

But Forster, characteristically, does not leave matters there, with some comparatively straightforward observation about the strains of existence and the possibility of a harmonious universe. In several passages, he opens up the question of what lies beyond the 'overarching sky'. For example, at the Bridge Party:

European costume had lighted like a leprosy. Few had yielded entirely, but none were untouched. There was a silence when he had finished speaking, on both sides of the court; at least, more ladies joined the English group, but their words seemed to die as soon as uttered. Some kites hovered overhead, impartial, over the kites passed the mass of a vulture, and, with an impartiality exceeding all, the sky, not deeply coloured but translucent, poured light from its whole circumference. It seemed unlikely that the series stopped here. Beyond the sky must not there be something that overarches all the skies, more impartial even than they? Beyond which again ... (pp. 59–60)

The scene of separation between the Anglo-Indians, confronting each other across the court, is enclosed with a description of the birds in the sky and the sky itself – but the birds are birds of prey. It is in this tension, where separation and unity interlock, that Forster insists the book remains – and even the sky may have something beyond it.

A great deal of critical attention has focused on Forster's characterization, and on the roles that his main characters perform in his novels. John Sayre Martin, for example, detects the motif of the journey in all the novels, whereby some characters experience something 'that lies beyond their normal range of activity and expectation', and are changed to some extent as a consequence. This pattern of change, however, is rather different from another type of development that is present. Forster himself, in *Aspects of the Novel*, states that a 'round' character is satisfying and interesting because it 'is capable of surprising [the reader] in a convincing way' (*Aspects of the Novel*, p. 81), thereby appearing to be as unpredictable as human beings themselves are. Taking his cue from this, Lionel Trilling comments on Forster's tendency to make his characters change, or act, in ways that counteract their previously ordained moral position in the novels:

He is always shocking us by removing the heroism of his heroes and heroines; in *A Passage to India*, Mrs Moore, of whom we had expected high actions, lets herself be sent away from the trial at which her testimony would have been crucial; Cyril Fielding, who as a solitary man had heroically opposed official ideas, himself becomes official when he is successful and married; and Dr Aziz cannot keep to his role of the sensitive and enlightened native.

Another criticism comes from John Beer, who comments on the

curious mixture of satire and collusive comedy in the characterization, which sometimes has the effect of charming the reader into imagining that Forster is genial.

Obviously, there is a range of different types of characterization in *A Passage to India*, as in many novels. There are the caricatured Anglo-Indians, who are not explored as personalities but are portrayed through their prejudices and social customs, the more fully delineated main characters, and even symbolic figures, such as the punkah-wallah in the courtroom, who is included by Forster to signify a life of instinct which has been ignored by Adela and her companions. *A Passage to India*, like all Forster's novels, tends towards being a 'novel of ideas', where even the main characters represent different ways of living and regarding life, and are part of the author's wider scheme. During the writing of the novel, as June Perry Levine has shown in a discussion of the manuscripts, Forster moved in the direction of generalizing his main characters; they may be said to represent qualities such as rationalism (Fielding), emotionalism (Aziz), or tranquillity (Godbole). Nevertheless, the main characters are by no means merely counters in a wider discussion. They give the impression of being 'round', in their ability to change, and Forster uses all his authorial omniscience to convey a great deal of information about them, filling in their histories and backgrounds, describing their thoughts and commenting on their feelings. In *Aspects of the Novel*, he says:

> The speciality of the novel is that the writer can talk about his characters as well as through them, or can arrange for us to listen when they talk to themselves. He has access to self-communings, and from that level he can descend even deeper and peer into the subconscious. A man does not talk to himself quite truly – not even to himself; the happiness or misery that he secretly feels proceed from causes that he cannot quite explain, because as soon as he raises them to the level of the explicable they lose their native quality. The novelist has a real pull here. He can show the subconscious short-circuiting straight into action ... he can also show it in its relation to soliloquy. (*Aspects of the Novel*, pp. 85–6)

All the main characters are given this authorial attention: we witness Adela's confusion before she enters the cave, Mrs Moore's experience in the cave, Fielding's frustration and disappointment when he has to choose between Aziz and the Anglo-Indian community, for example. Perhaps the best occasion is when Aziz mourns his wife briefly:

And, unlocking a drawer, he took out his wife's photograph. He gazed at it, and tears spouted from his eyes. He thought, 'How unhappy I am!' But because he really was unhappy another emotion soon mingled with his self-pity: he desired to remember his wife and could not. Why could he remember people whom he did not love? They were always so vivid to him, whereas the more he looked at this photograph the less he saw. She had eluded him thus, ever since they had carried her to her tomb. He had known that she would pass from his hands and eyes, but had thought she could live in his mind, not realizing that the very fact that we have loved the dead increases their unreality, and that the more passionately we invoke them the further they recede. A piece of brown cardboard and three children – that was all that was left of his wife. It was unbearable, and he thought again, 'How unhappy I am!' and became happier. He had breathed for an instant the mortal air that surrounds Orientals and all men, and he drew back from it with a gasp, for he was young. 'Never, never shall I get over this,' he told himself. 'Most certainly my career is a failure, and my sons will be badly brought up.' Since it was certain, he strove to avert it, and looked at some notes he had made on a case at the hospital. Perhaps some day a rich person might require this particular operation, and he gain a large sum. The notes interesting him on their own account, he locked the photograph up again. Its moment was over, and he did not think about his wife any more. (pp. 74–5)

We see Aziz feeling very unhappy and then, by degrees, cheering up. But Forster lets us understand a great deal more about the process than Aziz does himself, and he also conveys a sense of the irrationality of moods and changing feelings, in the way that Aziz turns to the medical notes and begins to forget his despondency. The passage combines generalizations on the enigma of grief with a depiction of Aziz moving from distress to unconcern as his attention is diverted; it is, perhaps, in Forster's terms, 'convincing', because it does not merely portray a conventional idea of mourning. In addition, the passage also demonstrates very closely Forster's habitual tendency to combine and elide a character's thoughts with his own statements. The sentence, 'Why could he remember people whom he did not love?' comes from Aziz, but the comment, 'the very fact that we have loved the dead increases their unreality' is Forster's.

This very distinctive mode of presenting character does not occur with all the main characters all the time. They are focused on, or recede, at different points in the novel, so that we do not know what Aziz feels during his imprisonment, or what Mrs Moore thinks as she is dying, for example. There is no single main character in *A*

Passage to India with whom the reader might identify, or who becomes the author's mouthpiece. In writing the novel, Forster deliberately rejected the convention of identification with one character, saying in a letter:

If you can pretend you can get inside one character, why not pretend it about all the characters? I see why. The illusion of life may vanish, and the creator degenerate into the showman. Yet some change of the sort must be made. The studied ignorance of novelists grows wearisome.

From this arises the feeling often expressed by readers and critics, that Forster's plots are disappointing. In *A Passage to India*, for example, we have become interested in the thoughts, feelings and dilemmas of Mrs Moore and Adela, only to find that both disappear from the novel after the trial.

While he was writing the novel, in 1922, Forster wrote in a letter to a friend that 'the characters are not sufficiently interesting for the atmosphere. This tempts me to emphasize the atmosphere, and so to produce a meditation rather than a drama.' However, he provides a range of different types of people, from the reactionary Mrs Turton and Callendar, through the main characters of Ronny, Adela, Fielding, Aziz, Mrs Moore and Godbole, to the members of the Indian community such as Hamidullah and the Nawab. Forster never provides a full physical description of his characters in the ways that, for example, Dickens and Hardy do. We are told of their appearance only in so far as it affects their personality and the way that they relate to others. Adela's plainness for example is clearly instrumental in producing her social awkwardness and earnestness, as well as being vital to the undercurrents at the Marabar Caves, where she meditates on the fact that neither she nor Ronny is physically attractive, while Aziz is. But instead, on the whole, much of the distinctiveness and variety of the characters in the novel is conveyed through their speech rhythms and phrases, which brilliantly express class, race and social attitude. Mrs Turton's superciliousness and assumption of status is reflected in her slang and lazy sentence structure when she says:

'It is only just five,' said Mrs Turton. 'My husband will be up from his office in a moment and start the thing. I have no idea what we have to do. It's the first time we've ever given a party like this at the Club. Mr Heaslop, when I'm dead and gone will you give parties like this? It's enough to make the old type of Burra Sahib turn in his grave.' (p. 59)

By contrast, we gain a sense of Aziz's sing-song inflection and

Oriental frame of mind, as well as his immediate enthusiasm and confidence, when he says,

'Then back with water streaming over you and perhaps rather a pain inside. But I did not mind. All my friends were paining with me. We have a proverb in Urdu: "What does unhappiness matter when we are all unhappy together?" which comes in conveniently after mangoes. Miss Quested, do wait for mangoes. Why not settle altogether in India?' (pp. 89–90)

This mode of characterization lends an interest to all the characters, major and minor. Forster's ability to capture inflection and social register is unerring. This also comes to the fore in his use of dialogue to convey characters in relationships. As in Jane Austen's novels, dialogue often expresses ironically the tensions, misunderstandings and inequalities between people. And, true to his theme of the necessity for friendship and love, Forster is as interested in the relationships between people as in the development of an individual. His use of dialogue is therefore sometimes comic and sometimes conveys depths of poignancy. Two examples will suffice. Ronny and Mrs Moore have several conversations in which they rehearse two very different attitudes towards British rule of India. Their conversations also convey the mother–son relationship, with all its traditional factors of authority, respect, criticism and impatience. The interchange,

'There's nothing in India but the weather, my dear mother; it's the alpha and omega of the whole affair.'
'Yes, as Mr McBryde was saying . . .'   (p. 68)

reveals how Mrs Moore understands that Ronny is mimicking his superiors, and how she gently but firmly reasserts her maternal authority, or at least, her right to his respect. We also see Ronny's condescension and fake knowingness, after only a short time in the country. A second example is from a series of conversations between Aziz and Fielding, who have tried hard to bridge cultural gaps and achieve friendship. However, their differences are conveyed strongly in the following dialogue:

'So you and Madamsell Adela used to amuse one another in the evening, naughty boy.'
Those drab and high-minded talks had scarcely made for dalliance. Fielding was so startled at the story being taken seriously, and so disliked being called a naughty boy, that he lost his head and cried: 'You little rotter! Well, I'm damned. Amusement indeed. Is it likely at such a time?'
'Oh, I beg your pardon, I'm sure. The licentious oriental imagination was

at work,' he replied, speaking gaily, but cut to the heart; for hours after his mistake he bled inwardly.   (p. 270)

The range of registers here is very great. Aziz attempts, slyly, to engage Fielding on an equal basis, but only succeeds in sounding offensive. Fielding reacts badly to being called a 'naughty boy' (he is, after all, a schoolmaster), and therefore delivers a doubly insulting epithet in 'You little rotter', a damning phrase which inadvertently underlines Aziz's racial 'inferiority'. Fielding's indignation is expressed in his characteristically dismissive 'Amusement indeed', which echoes his earlier 'Post-Impressionism, indeed!', and which assumes a tone of superiority and judgement. Aziz attempts to maintain a joking tone appropriate to equality by saying, as if in jest, 'The licentious oriental imagination was at work', but it is one of the prejudices against Indians held by the Anglo-Indians, and he seems to be struggling not to succumb to this insulting version of his race. Ironically, of course, the sexual tastes of Aziz and Fielding *are* quite different, as we have seen earlier in the novel. Through dialogue, vocabulary, and individual speech patterns, Forster has conveyed the respective personalities of Aziz and Fielding – Aziz's impulsiveness and insecurity, Fielding's bluffness and air of authority – and has also shown the difficulties of communication between people of different races and cultures.

The authorial voice

Analysis of the text demands a more detailed consideration of the voice or voices of the author within the narrative, and of the relationship which we, as readers, form with that voice. The question of the reader's relationship with the material of the story and with the implied author is crucial to any understanding of the narrative, and can only be formulated through close attention to the effects of the prose. The reader, that is to say, needs to be constantly alert to the shifting purposes of the prose at different times, and to the stylistic techniques utilized to gain these effects. *A Passage to India*, in the range and variety of its prose, and the ambitious reach of its geographic and metaphoric scope, requires the kind of close scrutiny which readers often reserve for the reading of poetry.

A Passage to India is, it might be claimed, concerned primarily with morality. It is therefore a text in which moral awareness (and moral blindness) is explored and foregrounded within a vividly realized external scene. While the reader will recall the drama of the central actions – the encounter in the mosque, Fielding's tea-party, the picnic at the caves, the trial, the Hindu festival – it will soon be realized that these external events depend upon, or lead to, other more inward 'events' – Adela's crisis, Mrs Moore's depression and withdrawal, Godbole's mystical ecstasy, and so on. In depicting inner and outer scenes Forster evinces masterly control of both omniscient and indirect narration. As he observed in *Aspects of the Novel*, 'The hidden life is, by definition, hidden . . . it is the function of the novelist to reveal the hidden life at its source' (pp. 55–6). Revelation is largely effected through free indirect speech which enacts the movements of the characters' thought in a fictional world where, as Forster wrily remarks, 'the secret life is visible' (*Aspects of the Novel*, p. 69). The points of inner debate and crisis remain firmly within the hands of the controlling author, and it is this 'speaker' who establishes the full moral perspective of the story as it unfolds. The question of the authorial voice must contain and include a disembodied intelligence that has access to the secrets of the characters and remains ubiquitous. The voice indeed seems to play a double role, becoming the characters at some points and edging away to claim separate identity at others. The widespread use of free indirect speech makes the texture of the novel highly dramatic and presentational; it gives the illusion of 'experienced speech' in relaying the thoughts of various characters. Forster can vary his voice from direct mimicry of a character's thought and speech to exposition of his own more wide-ranging vision. The 'voice' of *A Passage to India* is thus a dual one.

At no time in the course of the novel may we ignore the presence of the narrator in the story he tells. His voice represents what we may call subjectivity in language. Critics of fiction have tended to restrict questions about narrating technique to discussion of point of view, and this basically entails identifying the narrator with the author and the recipient with the reader. But of course the role of the narrator himself is fictive: the narrator of *A Passage to India* is not Forster, even where recognizably Forsterian opinions are advanced. The author/narrator knows and can describe the Club, Aziz's rooms, Fielding's house, the Rajah's palace; all Forster himself can do is to imagine them. The narrating situation is a complex whole in which everything must be transmitted in due order, and there is a very subtle interrelationship between narrating act, narrative levels and the sense of the 'person' invoked through the voice. No character in the novel, clearly, may contest with the narrator his privilege of ideological commentary. The narrator exerts a sovereign authority over his material through his penetrating voice.

The opening of the novel, which sets the scene before the reader, is a crucial instance of one kind of authorial voice within the text:

> Except for the Marabar Caves – and they are twenty miles off – the city of Chandrapore presents nothing extraordinary. Edged rather than washed by the river Ganges, it trails for a couple of miles along the bank, scarcely distinguishable from the rubbish it deposits so freely. There are no bathing-steps on the river front, as the Ganges happens not to be holy here; indeed there is no river front, and bazaars shut out the wide and shifting panorama of the stream. The streets are mean, the temples ineffective, and though a few fine houses exist they are hidden away in gardens or down alleys whose filth deters all but the invited guest. Chandrapore was never large or beautiful, but two hundred years ago it lay on the road between Upper India, then imperial, and the sea, and the fine houses date from that period. The zest for decoration stopped in the eighteenth century, nor was it ever democratic. In the bazaars there is no painting and scarcely any carving. The very wood seems made of mud, the inhabitants of mud moving. So abased, so monotonous is everything that meets the eye, that when the Ganges comes down it might be expected to wash the excrescence back into the soil. Houses do fall, people are drowned and left rotting, but the general outline of the town persists, swelling here, shrinking there, like some low but indestructible form of life. (p. 31)

This establishes, clearly enough, a setting, and the emphasis is upon muddle, upon life subsisting within an atmosphere of decay. Indeed, the very insignificance of Chandrapore seems to endow it with a curiously authentic significance. The paragraph is useful to the reader as information. At the same time there is a distinctively 'Forsterian' tone which may be readily identified, and which sets up the values to be explored in the text. The tone is that of a civilized, literate English observer. The narrator will not state so much as proceed by polite but barbed indirection. The city, for example, 'presents nothing extraordinary': the comment is polite, civilized, but imbued with a central irony which undermines the factual guide-book style. The words here seem to await connections which will give them deeper significance. The words 'nothing' and 'extraordinary', for instance, gain a new resonance in relation to the caves, as does the lack of carving in the bazaars. The description neatly illustrates the way the voice will move. The town is 'Edged rather than washed by the river Ganges', and the water itself is 'scarcely distinguishable from the rubbish'. After this remark we are hardly surprised to be told that the river 'happens not to be holy here'. Here the voice is self-evidently that of the outsider slightly mocking the Indian tendency to give religious connotations to any object or person, however improbable. The passage carefully draws the reader into a civilized collusion in its critique: 'The streets are mean, the temples ineffective.' The ineffectuality is aesthetic rather than religious, and India is presented as muddle rather than mystery. The narrator's allowance that there are 'a few fine houses' implies a certain privileged style of life in which invited guests might feature. The drily amused judgement about the 'zest for decoration' and its undemocratic nature gives the reader some useful information about the religious and social divisions of the sub-continent, but again from an outsider's point of view.

The passage is worth close interrogation. In its structure of feeling, in the implications of culture and value, the voice here is that of Cambridge. The writing, that is to say, represents the experience and expectations of a powerful social caste. The way the prose works may best be exemplified by placing it against another paragraph of descriptive material:

The small locomotive engine, Number 4, came clanking, stumbling down from Selston with seven full waggons. It appeared round the corner with loud threats of speed, but the colt that it startled from among the gorse, which still flickered indistinctly in the raw afternoon, out-distanced it at a canter. A woman, walking up the railway line to Underwood, drew back into the hedge, held her basket aside, and watched the footplate of the engine advancing. The trucks thumped heavily past, one by one, with slow inevitable movement, as she stood insignificantly trapped between the jolting black waggons and the hedge; then they curved away towards the coppice where the withered oak leaves dropped noiselessly, while the birds, pulling at the scarlet hips beside the track, made off into the dusk that had already crept into the spinney.

Here is a voice which, though equally assured in its aims and effects, clearly emanates from a different experience. This piece by D. H. Lawrence is full of nervous energy and closely observed detail. The language is demonstrative and energetic; it does not rest easily upon the shared class assumptions, the calling upon a known culture, which informs Forster's prose. While Forster's might be characterized as a prose of civilized intercourse, Lawrence's voice here is more explicitly spoken and dramatic, an articulation of response issuing from a wholly different sense of community.

On the problem of voice which such comparisons throw up,

Forster's own remarks are worthy of note. He argued, in *Aspects of the Novel*, that voice 'is the aspect of the novelist's work which asks to be read out loud, which appeals not to the eye, like most prose, but to the ear' (p. 51). A story can, he asserts, 'besides saying one thing after another', add something else, 'because of its connection with a voice' (p. 51). This added 'something', he warns, is not the author's personality; it is a transformation of the audience from readers into listeners in a discourse which takes us back to a tribal, orally-based situation. This is interesting. If it is true, then one must conclude that the 'tribal' audience for Forster is a privileged one, and this privilege is everywhere implied in the beautifully held tone of *A Passage to India*. In this work, more clearly than elsewhere in Forster, potentially controversial material is in some senses defused by the civilizing ironic voice which draws the reader into an easy assent. This highly effective opening paragraph sets out to establish the coexistence within an ironic vision of the elements of the bizarre, the beautiful and the muddled. The suggestion of the entire chapter is that all this multitudinous life is, however unrelated, finally contained by the vastness of the Indian sky. The Forsterian voice generalizes, comments, occasionally dogmatizes; but it always cunningly preserves the reader's acceptance of the stance and the valuation. The ideology of the text, enshrined in the voice, is at the same time both covert and stated.

A passage which nicely exemplifies the narrator's expertise in controlling the reader's response, and in moving from third person into free indirect speech and out again, is the description, in Chapter IV, of the Christian missionaries who 'never came up to the Club'. Having described in conventionally omniscient terms the reactions of the Indian community to the Collector's Bridge Party, the focus shifts cleverly and more intimately to the two humble missionaries and their attitude to the question of invitations:

All invitations must proceed from heaven perhaps; perhaps it is futile for men to initiate their own unity, they do but widen the gulfs between them by the attempt. So at all events thought old Mr Graysford and young Mr Sorley, the devoted missionaries who lived out beyond the slaughter-houses, always travelled third on the railways, and never came up to the Club. In our Father's house are many mansions, they taught, and there alone will the incompatible multitudes of mankind be welcomed and soothed. Not one shall be turned away by the servants on that veranda, be he black or white, not one shall be kept standing who approaches with a loving heart. And why should the divine hospitality cease here? Consider, with all reverence, the monkeys. May there not be a mansion for the monkeys also? Old Mr Graysford said No, but young Mr Sorley, who was advanced, said Yes; he saw no reason why monkeys should not have their collateral share of bliss, and he had sympathetic discussions about them with his Hindu friends. And the jackals? Jackals were indeed less to Mr Sorley's mind, but he admitted that the mercy of God, being infinite, may well embrace all mammals. And the wasps? He became uneasy during the descent to wasps, and was apt to change the conversation. And oranges, cactuses, crystals and mud? And the bacteria inside Mr Sorley? No, no, this is going too far. We must exclude someone from our gathering, or we shall be left with nothing. (p. 58)

The effects here are complex: the missionaries are both admired and satirized in their relation to life. The narrator remains firmly in control, and the tone balances precariously between endorsement and satire of the missionaries' philosophy. The respectful tone of 'Not one shall be turned away by the servants on that veranda, be he black or white, not one shall be kept standing who approaches with a loving heart', oscillates with the satire concerning Mr Sorley who 'was advanced'. The notion of the monkeys having their 'collateral share of bliss', if philosophically admirable, sounds a note of comedy in its phrasing, and exposes the innocent naïvety of the missionaries' character. This tone continues in the 'descent to wasps' and bacteria. The final sentence treads a knife-edge between authorial commentary and free indirect speech, while raising again the central question of exclusion.

Within these passages, and throughout the novel, there is an effect of mastery and command which is quietly and unemphatically located in the language. During the act of reading, the audience undergo an alteration; this alteration is wrought through the thoughts of another, whom for convenience we characterize as 'E. M. Forster'. Through such operations we are granted, as readers, the experience of thinking thoughts, possessing experiences, foreign to ourselves. We are subject to ideas which are not our own; through the potency of the language we possess them. Such thoughts include a wide range of consciousnesses, and constitute what we may normally think of as the 'fictional world' of the novel. Yet they do not entail that feeling we may normally have of separation of our thought processes from the concrete world around us. On the contrary, in the experiences recounted through the novel we feel totally attuned to everything surrounding us. Although we recognize the encounter at the mosque, the tea-party, the visit to the

Marabar, the scene at the Club and so forth as 'objects' presented to us by another subject, we experience them (such is the power of the text) as if they were our own. We live, in the act of reading, within a certain type of identity with the book. The authorial voice in *A Passage to India* commands a wide reach and scope. Forster is impressively ventriloquial in allowing the reader access to such a variety of imagined experience and consciousness. He is enabled, through the third-person stance, to close and to distance himself from such characters as Aziz, Fielding, Adela and Mrs Moore.

We might take Mrs Moore's reflections upon her experience in the cave as a case in point:

> The crush and the smells she could forget, but the echo began in some indescribable way to undermine her hold on life. Coming at a moment when she chanced to be fatigued, it had managed to murmur: 'Pathos, piety, courage – they exist, but are identical, and so is filth. Everything exists, nothing has value.' . . . suddenly, at the edge of her mind, Religion appeared, poor little talkative Christianity, and she knew that all its divine words from 'Let there be light' to 'It is finished' only amounted to 'boum'. Then she was terrified over an area larger than usual; the universe, never comprehensible to her intellect, offered no repose to her soul, the mood of the last two months took definite form at last, and she realized that she didn't want to write to her children, didn't want to communicate with anyone, not even with God. (pp. 160–61)

The seminal importance of this passage lies in its poised awareness and registration of reflection available to the character and to the narrator. Forster claimed of the narrator of fiction, 'He has access to self-communings, and from that level he can descend even deeper and peer into the subconscious' (*Aspects of the Novel*, p. 85). When the echo says 'Everything exists, nothing has value', we may read it as the experience of an elderly lady; but it of course reverberates into the entire world of the novel with a radical effect of unsettlement. The liberal-humanist project endorsed in Forster's literary work is undermined here, and the undermining is foregrounded in the oracular and poetic language which strains the realist discourse. Julia Kristeva has interestingly suggested that 'poetic' language is 'unsettled' because it reactivates instinctive, maternal elements of the personality which are suppressed when the individual becomes a linguistic subject. Such language as that employed by Forster here, and in the description of the Hindu festival, may therefore be indicative of instinctive drives repressed by the ego. Yet this unsettlement is held within a framework of 'knowledge' by the narrative voice, a voice which, as Forster argues, gives us 'the illusion of perspicacity and of power' (*Aspects of the Novel*, p. 70). The narrator cannily never allows the narrative here to expand disastrously into philosophical generality of the kind which characterizes and mars the novels, for instance, of George Meredith, by whom Forster was deeply influenced. We remain 'anchored' within Mrs Moore, registering and partly sharing her terror.

At other more relaxed moments the prose is equally successful, for example, in registering, enacting and simultaneously judging the mercurial temperament of Aziz, as when he gazes fondly at his dead wife's photograph:

It was unbearable, and he thought again, 'How unhappy I am!' and became happier. He had breathed for an instant the mortal air that surrounds Orientals and all men, and he drew back from it with a gasp, for he was young. 'Never, never shall I get over this,' he told himself. 'Most certainly my career is a failure, and my sons will be badly brought up.' Since it was certain, he strove to avert it, and looked at some notes he had made on a case at the hospital. Perhaps some day a rich person might require this particular operation, and he gain a large sum. The notes interesting him on their own account, he locked the photograph up again. Its moment was over, and he did not think about his wife any more. (p. 75)

The narrative acts judgementally here in placing the young Indian, as in the comment about the 'mortal air'. At the same time it amusingly dramatizes the shifts and plunges of Aziz's mind, with his wholly credible switch from private grief to fantasies of wealth. Aziz, and indeed all the characters, are not portrayed in the manner of Virginia Woolf, as separate consciousnesses, but as social beings 'tirelessly occupied with human relationships' (*Aspects of the Novel*, p. 63). Like much realist fiction, *A Passage to India* insists upon the essential connectedness of all human beings. 'Only connect', the motto of *Howards End*, might equally well have been placed at the head of this novel. Each character has relationships and responsibilities which they have created, or found themselves in. The structure of the novel, and particularly the movement of the prose, works to make meaningful the relations between the individual and the community. The characters are presented in relation to natural, psychological, moral and religious laws which are interrelated. Life in this muddlesome and mysterious sub-continent can only be meaningful and coherent if perceived through relationship and connection, and in fiction such sense of connection is wrought through the voice.

The problematic of relationships centres in the sense Forster possesses of an essential unknowability in each individual running counter to the liberal desire for, and necessity of, communication. This unknowability is registered as more challenging in cases of extreme difference – between classes, between sexes, or even, as in *A Passage to India*, between races. In the sense that all voices are the author's, it is the dialogue through which Forster explores most immediately and dramatically the divides and bridges between people. In its command of register, rhythm and linguistic divergence the authorial voice of *A Passage to India* is indisputably successful in giving the reader a wide variety of conversational discourse. This variety may be illustrated by examining the subtle differentiation between dialogue involving social and racial equals and dialogue where the participants are notably unequal. Near the beginning of the novel we encounter Aziz among his Muslim friends, and as ever the conversation turns to the British rulers; Hamidullah and Mahmoud Ali are debating the point:

'You fellows will not believe me, but I have driven with Turton in his carriage – Turton! Oh yes, we were once quite intimate. He has shown me his stamp collection.'

'He would expect you to steal it now. Turton! But red-nosed boy will be far worse than Turton!'

'I do not think so. They all become exactly the same – not worse, not better. I give any Englishman two years, be he Turton or Burton. It is only the difference of a letter. And I give any Englishwoman six months. All are exactly alike. Do you not agree with me?'

'I do not,' replied Mahmoud Ali, entering into the bitter fun, and feeling both pain and amusement at each word that was uttered. 'For my own part I find such profound differences among our rulers. Red-nose mumbles, Turton talks distinctly, Mrs Turton takes bribes, Mrs Red-nose does not and cannot, because so far there is no Mrs Red-nose.'

'Bribes?'

'Did you not know that when they were lent to Central India over a canal scheme some rajah or other gave her a sewing machine in solid gold so that the water should run through his state?' (p. 34)

The passage beautifully catches the slightly comic strain which is felt by people communicating in an alien, colonial language. The claim for intimacy with Turton is unconsciously demolished by the stamp collection; the phrase 'red-nosed boy will be ...' enacts a mistaken usage which neatly marks out the secondary status of Indians in their own country. There is a sense in which this scene of dialogue displays serious engagement with profound issues

of international relationships, but also and equally it displays
intimacy, closeness and good-fellowship which the voice of the
novelist marvellously brings to life. Throughout the novel, indeed,
the dialogue crackles with energy and wit, and the authorial voice
follows the switchbacks of emotion by tiny and cunningly imagined
linguistic details. These broken rhythms which so closely knit
together internal and external action may be observed, for example,
when Adela and Ronny, having agreed not to marry, converse and
are then interrupted by the Nawab Bahadur:

> 'Do you know what the name of that green bird up above us is?' she
> asked, putting her shoulder rather nearer to his.
> 'Bee-eater.'
> 'Oh no, Ronny, it has red bars on its wings.'
> 'Parrot,' he hazarded.
> 'Good gracious, no.' ...
> 'McBryde has an illustrated bird-book,' he said dejectedly. 'I'm no good
> at all at birds, in fact I'm useless at any information outside my own job.
> It's a great pity.'
> 'So am I. I'm useless at everything.'
> 'What do I hear?' shouted the Nawab Bahadur at the top of his voice,
> causing both of them to start. 'What most improbable statement have I
> heard? An English lady useless? No, no, no, no, no.' He laughed genially,
> sure, within limits, of his welcome.
> 'Hullo, Nawab Bahadur! Been watching the polo again?' said Ronny
> tepidly.   (p. 101)

The tiny cameo exactly catches many of the unnerving nuances
of interracial contact in a colonial country. The tepidity of the
lovers' conversation is convincingly 'English' in its renunciation of
emotion, and there is a sense of racial collusion as the young
couple encounter the hospitable but slightly absurd Nawab with his
distinctive linguistic and gestural repertoire. Ronny's indifference
to the natural life of India is part of the Raj's deliberate blindness
and Eurocentrism, with its false emphasis on his 'job'. His sense of
'pity' is clearly unfelt, and the entire conversation dramatically
makes manifest Forster's theme of the 'undeveloped heart'. If
Ronny hides within a racial stereotype, so too does the Nawab, his
social uncertainty issuing in his shouting intervention and his forced
geniality. Only Adela, genuinely inquisitive about Indian life, does
not retreat behind a known range of language responses to the
situation.

The voice (or range of voices) in the novel is nowhere heard more spellbindingly than in the scene of Fielding's tea-party, which the narrative implicitly balances against the Collector's Bridge Party. It is significant, perhaps, that this should be so, since in some senses Fielding is certainly Forster's avatar in the novel, the character closest to assuming the Forsterian voice. In the first encounter between Fielding and Aziz there is to be found a deeply persuasive assumption of roles on the part of the novelist, an assumption which actively sets before the reader the risks and rewards involved in cultural exchange. The two men immediately fraternize informally, with Fielding still dressing after a bath:

> 'Guess what I look like before you come out. That will be a kind of game.'
> 'You're five feet nine inches high,' said Fielding, surmising this much through the ground glass of the bedroom door.
> 'Jolly good. What next? Have I not a venerable white beard?'
> 'Blast!'
> 'Anything wrong?'
> 'I've stamped on my last collar-stud.'
> 'Take mine, take mine.'
> 'Have you a spare one?'
> 'Yes, yes, one minute.'
> 'Not if you're wearing it yourself.'
> 'No, no, one in my pocket.' Stepping aside, so that his outline might vanish, he wrenched off his collar, and pulled out of his shirt the back stud, a gold stud, which was part of a set that his brother-in-law had brought him from Europe. 'Here it is,' he cried.
> 'Come in with it if you don't mind the unconventionality.' (p. 82)

The exchanges, direct, friendly and intimate, are sealed by the offer of the stud: through such tiny incidents does the narrative imagine and project connection. The conversation proceeds famously, and Fielding notes 'the liveliness with which the younger generation handled a foreign tongue' (p. 83). Aziz expatiates romantically upon the Mogul emperors, but then the conversation suddenly teeters on the edge of disaster:

> 'You can talk to Miss Quested about the Peacock Throne if you like – she's artistic, they say.'
> 'Is she a Post-Impressionist?'
> 'Post-Impressionism, indeed! Come along to tea. This world is getting too much for me altogether.'
> Aziz was offended. The remark suggested that he, an obscure Indian, had no right to have heard of Post-Impressionism – a privilege reserved for the Ruling Race, that. He said stiffly, 'I do not consider Mrs Moore my friend, I only met her accidentally in my mosque,' and was adding, 'A single meeting

is too short to make a friend,' but before he could finish the sentence the stiffness vanished from it, because he felt Fielding's fundamental goodwill. (p. 84)

The narrative voice here moves with fine decorum between the two men, tracing their closeness and antipathies in an ever-changing dialectic of verbal and emotional gesture. The entire scene conveys to the reader a world made up of a multiplicity of viewpoints and interpretations, and this range widens with the advent of the two women and Professor Godbole. The interplay of dialogue and commentary in this seminal episode exposes the fissures in the racial landscape with economy and wit, and reaches a climax after Aziz's foolhardy invitation to the caves. The party seek enlightenment about the nature of the Marabar from the Hindu professor:

'They are immensely holy, no doubt,' said Aziz, to help on the narrative.
'Oh no, oh no.'
'Still, they are ornamented in some way.'
'Oh no.'
'Well, why are they so famous? We all talk of the famous Marabar Caves. Perhaps that is our empty brag.'
'No, I should not quite say that.'
'Describe them to this lady, then.'
'It will be a great pleasure.' He forewent the pleasure, and Aziz realized that he was keeping back something about the caves. He realized because he often suffered from similar inhibitions himself. (p. 92)

The voice of the narrator traces the underlying struggle of Muslim and Hindu with impressive sympathy. Adela, we are told, 'did not know that the comparatively simple mind of the Mohammedan was encountering Ancient Night'. The intervention of Ronny, irritable and insensitive, speaks for itself of the impact of the Raj on ancient civilizations and courtesies. By ranging through the worldly geniality of Fielding, the genuine curiosity of the two women, Aziz's enthusiastic banter, Godbole's enigmatic silences, and Ronny's bristling anger, the novelist's voice in this scene puts the reader in possession of a wide range of views about India, and perhaps about human nature. The voice works successfully by not endorsing any single point of view to the exclusion of others. Taken together, the voices in the scene provide evidence of the search for truth. If, in the caves sequence, the reader is left to flounder in a world where all values are relatively worthless, in the tea-party scene there is an assumption of truth which may be reached through sympathy and goodwill. Each voice, each character possesses, through the manipulative prowess of the authorial voice, what has been termed 'creatural dignity'. Forster, we might say, has observed the Jamesian edict that the novelist should saturate himself in the imagined life of his characters. Such a degree of immersion endows the characters with a life which is animated through language and idiom. The narrative, indeed, exhibits an almost Wildean facility which hits off character and culture with telling force. Such phrases as Dr Panna Lal's 'I was mislaid', Nawab Bahadur's 'Half one league onwards', Aziz's response to Mrs Moore, 'Then we are in the same box', or the Indian lady's recital, 'Eastbourne, Piccadilly, High Park Corner', serve both to mirror and to create character and milieu. On the other side Fielding's hasty 'Post-Impressionism, indeed!', Mrs McBryde's 'Oh, Nancy, how topping', or Mrs Turton's exclamation at the Bridge Party, 'Why, they speak English', reinforce and dramatize the nature of the gulf between the communities.

The voice of *A Passage to India*, with its wide-ranging mastery and scrupulous observance of linguistic nuance, proves to be an ideal vehicle for the material. Yet it remains trapped within its own ideology. The authorial voice, liberal, humane, agnostic, implies in every sentence of the book the Bloomsbury values of culture and human relationships. The stance and tone, sympathetic, ironic and unified, issue from a class position which remains assured in every crisis of the plot. Indeed, the crises appear to be imagined, like the trial, to endorse the unitary values implied by the narrative voice. The novel possesses a homogeneity of utterance which had been markedly absent from Forster's earlier novels. The achieved nature of this voice, and the centrality of the vision it propounds, cannot wholly conceal the inflections of the ruling-class mandarin dialect. However, at the climactic points this 'Cambridge' voice, elsewhere so resonantly confident and disarmingly relaxed, betrays a sense of strain which helps to unmask and confront its own ideology:

Professor Godbole had never mentioned an echo; it never impressed him, perhaps. There are some exquisite echoes in India; there is the whisper round the dome at Bijapur; there are the long, solid sentences that voyage through the air at Mandu, and return unbroken to their creator. The echo in a Marabar cave is not like these, it is entirely devoid of distinction. Whatever is said, the same monotonous noise replies, and quivers up and down the walls until it is absorbed into the roof. 'Boum' is the sound as far as the human alphabet can express it, or 'bou-oum', or 'ou-boum' – utterly dull. Hope, politeness, the blowing of a nose, the squeak of a boot, all produce 'boum'. Even the striking of a match starts a little worm coiling, which is too small to complete a circle, but is eternally watchful. And if several people talk at once an overlapping howling noise begins, echoes generate echoes, and the cave is stuffed with a snake composed of small snakes, which writhe independently. (pp. 158–9)

As the party had approached the hills, we are told how the precipices rose above them, 'bland and bold'. In the description of the echo the voice challenges the blandly unifying strategy of its own procedure and simultaneously seeks to compel the reader to accept the inadequacy of his or her knowledge. There is uncertainty here, mirrored in the stylistic disjunctions, the class-based English superiority of 'some exquisite echoes' descending into the guide-book catalogue of echoes, and then changing into the apocalyptic tone of the second half of the paragraph. The unifying narrative voice, which implies value and rationality, is nullified and muffled by the echo it describes. The perceptual and conceptual categories on which Western thought is based are negated by the pervasive echo, and the liberal-humanist project of connections falters in the uncertainty of its verbal expression, an expression which envisages and enacts its own destruction. The text momentarily contemplates disintegration, before 'placing' this experience within the mind of a single character, Mrs Moore. Such a passage, with its abrupt reversals of meaning, suspends both reader and text on the brink of non-meaning.

A different but related effect is produced in the poetic description of Professor Godbole's mystical ecstasy during the Hindu festival towards the end of the novel:

Godbole consulted the music-book, said a word to the drummer, who broke rhythm, made a thick little blur of sound, and produced a new rhythm. This was more exciting, the inner images it evoked more definite, and the singers' expressions became fatuous and languid. They loved all men, the whole universe, and scraps of their past, tiny splinters of detail, emerged for a moment to melt into the universal warmth. Thus Godbole, though she was not important to him, remembered an old woman he had met in Chandrapore days. Chance brought her into his mind while it was in this heated state, he did not select her, she happened to occur among the throng of soliciting images, a tiny splinter, and he impelled her by his spiritual force to that place where completeness can be found. Completeness, not reconstruction. His senses grew thinner, he remembered a wasp seen he forgot where, perhaps on a stone. He loved the wasp equally, he impelled it likewise, he was imitating God. And the stone where the wasp clung – could he . . . (pp. 283–4)

In attempting to articulate so alien an experience the narrative voice strains at its furthest limits. The sensitive and the humane, the site of the liberal values projected by the voice, all this is undermined and challenged in ways which illumine the contradictions in the text's ideology. The effect of the prose at this point in the story is of loss of control and continuity, of shock to the reader which is only contained with difficulty by the authorial voice. The alien universe which is imagined enshrines a sense of loss of self on the part of both narrator and reader which might usefully be related to Roland Barthes' concept of *jouissance*, a sense of joyful pleasure which occurs wherever there is radical disruption, a gap opened up between the reader's (and the author's) historical and cultural presuppositions and the feeling of a text directly felt as a sensory experience. At such a disjuncture, Barthes would argue, the reader 'at once takes pleasure, through the text, in the consistency of his self and its fall'. The discrepancies and contradictions of the Forsterian text here, the strained nature of the poetic voice, represents an attack on the authority of language as rational discourse which sets this mystical ecstasy beyond what Bloomsbury, concerned with what Forster termed 'the life of values', could know or transcribe. The authorial voice momentarily wavers, becomes dewesternized and depersonalized. Ultimately it retreats back into the knowable communities of Aziz and Fielding, where its scope is commanding and effortless. If the voice of *A Passage to India*, speaking from a centre of power, manipulates and persuades the reader across a wide tract of experience, its poetic 'faking' (as Forster named it in *Aspects of the Novel*) is profoundly revealing of a countervailing impulse towards doubt and self-contradiction, a dismantling of that self lovingly constructed by Western rationalist culture.

Structure

The division of *A Passage to India* into three parts is so deliberately noticeable that the reader soon recognizes the necessity to consider what its significance may be. This simple challenge becomes a kind of acrostic: the reader is tempted into interpreting the meanings of 'Mosque', 'Caves', and 'Temple', and reading those meanings into the effect of the novel as a whole. Forster himself provided an additional 'clue' by later revealing that the three parts 'also represent the three seasons of the Cold Weather, the Hot Weather, and the

Rains, which divide the Indian year'. Once we begin to consider the novel in this way, the conscious artistry and patterning become evident. They are not merely an intriguing feature which playfully leads the reader into another level of interpretation – although the expansion of thematic and symbolic meaning is achieved through them, as will be shown later. There are several kinds of ordering in *A Passage to India*, and their prominence reveals Forster's conviction that the art of the novel is important. In reading Forster's fiction, it is helpful to remember that for Forster the story is regrettably necessary, while the 'pattern' and 'rhythm' in a novel are a noble and significant dimension. In *Aspects of the Novel*, he says,

Yes – oh dear yes – the novel tells a story. That is the fundamental aspect without which it could not exist. That is the highest factor common to all novels, and I wish that it was not so, that it could be something different – melody, or perception of the truth, not this low atavistic form ... It runs like a backbone – or may I say a tapeworm, for its beginning and end are arbitrary. (pp. 40, 41)

In contrast to the 'tapeworm' of a story, the shaping of the novel as a whole, which Forster calls pattern, produces a sense of beauty. An internal technique of 'repetition plus variation'(*Aspects of the Novel*, p. 149), which he calls rhythm, provides a 'lovely waxing and waning to fill us with surprise and freshness and hope' (*Aspects of the Novel*, p. 148). Ultimately, this emphasis derives from Forster's faith in art to produce order and meaning in the midst of confusing and often depressing life.

A Passage to India has both pattern and rhythm, in Forster's terms. It is shaped into three sections, which are given titles and are distinguished from one another in location and mood. Themes, symbols and phrases are all repeated, echoed and varied throughout the novel. There is less of a narrative thread than a series of repetitions: in other words, the narrative does not just follow one sequence of events, but, like contrapuntal and symphonic music, develops a number of motifs, or themes, which interweave and create meaning. Peter Burra described this as

the use of *leit-motif* phrases and images to link up separated parts, with the additional function of dramatic irony and symbolism. This it is which gives pattern to the most diffuse of all forms. This device – of *motifs*, irony, and symbols – is, in fact, the modern equivalent of the classical unities, an invention of the greatest value, having all the classical advantages and none of their so severe limitations.

At one point in *Aspects of the Novel*, Forster appears to be describing the structure of *A Passage to India*:

Is there any effect in novels comparable to the effect of the Fifth Symphony as a whole, where, when the orchestra stops, we hear something that has never actually been played? The opening movement, the andante, and the trio-scherzo-trio-finale-trio-finale that composes the third block, all enter the mind at once, and extend one another into a common entity. This common entity, this new thing, is the symphony as a whole, and it has been achieved mainly (though not entirely) by the relation between the three big blocks of sound which the orchestra has been playing. I am calling this relation 'rhythmic'. (*Aspects of the Novel*, p. 149)

The 'three big blocks of sound' would seem to parallel the three parts of *A Passage to India*, and Forster's quest for a 'common entity' is also evident in the texture of repetition and variation which lasts in the reader's mind beyond the end of the novel. Forster goes on to say, in *Aspects of the Novel*, 'in music fiction is likely to find its nearest parallel' (p. 149). He has already spoken of hourglass and 'grand chain' shapes when describing pattern. And in an interview in 1952, he explained the presence of the 'Temple' section in *A Passage to India* as 'architecturally necessary. I needed a lump, or a Hindu temple if you like – a mountain standing up. It is well placed; and it gathers up some strings.' What is very noticeable is that analogies from the other arts – for example, music, pictorial art, or architecture – seem to be needed in order to describe this aspect of the novel. In this sense, the shape, patterning and structure of the novel are apart from any meaning or plot that can be summarized or recounted. E. K. Brown talks of the reader's experience of this aspect of the novel as passing 'beyond character, story, and setting, [to] attend, delightedly, to the grouping and ungrouping of ideas and emotions'. The patterning of symbol and motif is often not explicitly connected with the characters or the story, but exists in an area of the novel which is available only to the author and his readers. Instead of authorial comment, however, the parallels or connections which are created by juxtaposition or repetition are what convey certain meanings to the reader here.

These, then, are features which resemble a Symbolist aesthetic in many ways, and which indicate the modernity of the novel. Frank Kermode comments that 'We, in our time, are ... incapable of genuinely supposing a work of art to be something quite different from *A Passage to India*; it is, in this sense, contemporary and exemplary'. The topic of structure touches very closely the uses of symbolism and irony in *A Passage to India*, and more detailed discussions of particular symbols and of ironic twists to plot and character will follow in later sections. It is important to note here, though, that the symbolic and thematic references to the 'echo' in the Marabar Caves are cleverly mirrored in the structure and linguistic texture of the novel itself. As Lionel Trilling says,

the very texture of the story is a reticulation of echoes. Actions and speeches return, sometimes in a better, sometimes in a worse form, given back by the perplexing 'arch' of the Indian universe.

Not only is the word 'echo' itself repeated in numerous contexts, but other phrases and idioms are 'echoed'. This provides thematic parallels, of course. It also draws the shape and diversity of the novel tightly together, so that references across, forwards, and backwards in the text accumulate. And in a novel where one of the central experiences is of a cave where,

Whatever is said, the same monotonous noise replies, and quivers up and down the walls until it is absorbed into the roof. 'Boum' is the sound as far as the human alphabet can express it, or 'bou-oum', or 'ou-boum' – utterly dull. Hope, politeness, the blowing of a nose, the squeak of a boot, all produce 'boum' (p. 159)

then the repetition of words and phrases within the text accretes significance, mirroring the subject, of 'meaning', in the form of expression. Forster asks the reader to *listen* attentively and imaginatively to his novel.

Some examples from the novel will be helpful here. The sound of the train taking the party to the Marabar Caves is repetitive: it comes to represent, perhaps, the monotonous pattern of Indian life opposed to the directed purposefulness of Adela in her Anglo-Indian phase:

her thoughts ever veered to the manageable future, and to the Anglo-Indian life she had decided to endure. And, as she appraised it with its adjuncts of Turtons and Burtons, the train accompanied her sentences, 'pomper, pomper', the train half asleep, going nowhere in particular and with no passenger of importance in any of its carriages, the branch-line train, lost on a low embankment between dull fields. (p. 148)

The reader may, with the benefit of a second or subsequent reading, appreciate the ominousness of Adela's physical and aural surroundings. There is yet another repetition in the passage, as well: the 'Turtons and Burtons' here repeat the exasperated Indian point of view, ' "They all become exactly the same – not worse, not better. I give any Englishman two years, be he Turton or Burton" ' (p. 34). This minor echo functions to reinforce the other monotony, of British rule in India, which Adela 'had decided to endure'. The phrase is echoed at the end of the novel, when Aziz cries, ' "Clear out, all you Turtons and Burtons" ' (p. 314).

Forster is also fond of suggesting by this technique emotional affinities between characters who do not necessarily know each other very well. The most famous example in *A Passage to India* is the connection of the wasp with Mrs Moore in Godbole's mind, which will be discussed in the section on symbolism. A similar example, though, is when Mrs Moore's statement to Ronny, ' "God ... is ... love" ' (p. 70), is repeated in the inscription in the Hindu temple: 'God si Love' (p. 283). It is a fairly common sentiment, but it gains interest here in the comic misspelling, which seems to convey both the lack of inhibition in the Hindu rites and the poignant misuse of an alien tongue. It also once again links Mrs Moore's cast of mind with the Indian perspective on life.

Sometimes, in this novel which is obsessed with 'mystery', the vital steps of the plot are ignored by the authorial voice, and may only be discerned through the pattern and repetition. Adela's state of mind at two crucial points is conveyed through her perception of two similar sets of marks. She consents to marry Ronny, it seems, because of the excitement of the accident in the Nawab's car, where

Steady and smooth ran the marks of the car, ribbons neatly nicked with lozenges; then all went mad ... Adela in her excitement knelt and swept her skirts about, until it was she if anyone who appeared to have attacked the car. The incident was a great relief to them both. They forgot their abortive personal relationship, and felt adventurous as they muddled about in the dust. (p. 104)

It is interesting that even in this passage, there are intimations of central concerns: the association of Adela with an 'attack', and the reference to 'muddle'. Just before she enters the cave where she will feel attacked, she reaches a realization that is prompted by the same pattern:

The rock was nicked by a double row of footholds, and somehow the question was suggested by them. Where had she seen footholds before? Oh yes, they were the pattern traced in the dust by the wheels of the Nawab Bahadur's car. She and Ronny – no, they did not love each other. (p. 162)

Despite the deliberate mysteriousness of what actually happens in the cave, most readers conclude that the recognition that she is marrying without love generates some kind of hysterical reaction on Adela's part. The pattern on the ground encourages attraction the first time and repulsion the second time: this is also echoed on a larger scale when Adela is exorcised of her 'echo' by reliving the excursion at the trial, the experience of the cave causing disorientation the first time and clarity the second time.

Finally, the structuring of the novel overall, through repetition and irony, may be demonstrated by the simple example of Aziz's approving remark, ' "Then you are an Oriental" ' (pp. 45, 306), first of all to Mrs Moore, and two years later, to her son. It could be seen as one of the most optimistic indications in the novel: that despite all his bitterness and withdrawal from the British, Aziz still responds from his heart when he meets someone he feels affinity with. Yet there is also a sense in which this repetition reminds the reader of what happened after the first meeting between Aziz and Mrs Moore: the tense tea-party, the efforts to be friends, which led Aziz into such deep water.

The structure of *A Passage to India*, once the reader begins to investigate, becomes a highly complex vehicle for the transmission of layers and nuances of meaning, and these accumulate with increased familiarity with the novel. As Peter Burra says,

Mr Forster has developed the art of clues and chains to an unusual extent. In its simplest form it consists of throwing in hints that are a preparation for events that follow probably much later. They are generally so casually introduced that we hardly observe them; hence a full appreciation of his novels depends absolutely on a second reading.

The symbolism of the novel

Literary symbolism may be variously defined. It clearly involves the use of concrete imagery to express abstract ideas and emotions. It is, in the words of the French poet Mallarmé, 'the act of choosing an object or extracting from it a "state of the soul" '. The extraction process, he went on, worked 'by a series of decipherings'. In symbolic writing, as the German poet Goethe had argued many years earlier, idea is translated into image, but 'in such a way that the idea still remains infinitely active and inaccessible in the image so that, even expressed in all languages, it remains inexpressible'. It is the power of the symbol, as another German romantic put it, 'that the representation and what is represented, in constant mutual exchange, incite and constrain the mind to linger and to penetrate more deeply'. Ideas are suggested instantaneously through a symbol; the art of symbolism is the art of expressing feelings, not through direct description or definition, but by recreating feelings in the mind of the reader through the use of unexplained symbols. Indeed, symbolism may serve to create a sense of a world 'beyond' reality, to transform the reader's sense of that reality. The French symbolist poets, under Mallarmé's tutelage, aimed at producing linguistic effects which worked like music, and this project is shared, in the more mundane art of the novel, by Forster:

> Music, though it does not employ human beings, though it is governed by intricate laws, nevertheless does offer in its final expression a type of beauty which fiction might achieve in its own way. Expansion. That is the idea the novelist must cling to. Not completion. Not rounding off but opening out. When the symphony is over we feel that the notes and tunes composing it have been liberated, they have found in the rhythm of the whole their individual freedom. Cannot the novel be like that? Is not there something of it in *War and Peace*? – the book with which we began and in which we must end. Such an untidy book. Yet, as we read it, do not great chords begin to sound behind us, and when we have finished does not every item . . . lead a larger existence than was possible at the time? (*Aspects of the Novel*, pp. 149–50)

If all art aspired to the condition of music, then Forster, Virginia Woolf and others felt that the novel should not stray behind. To get beyond a surface reality there is discernible, in *A Passage to India* or *To the Lighthouse*, a fusion of images and a sense of musical structure and patterning. Symbolism is a dual concept: it suggests both that reality is only a façade which conceals emotions within the writer and that there is an ideal world towards which human beings aspire. Both elements are to be found in *A Passage to India*.

'Yes – oh dear yes – the novel tells a story', Forster reluctantly concedes in *Aspects of the Novel* (p. 40). At the same time he insists that fiction possesses 'nobler aspects' (p. 42). These aspects might be indicated by recalling a comment Forster made about *A Passage to India* during the 1950s:

> the book is not really about politics, though it is the political aspect of it that caught the general public and made it sell. It's about something wider than politics, about the search of the human race for a more lasting home, about the universe as embodied in the Indian earth and the Indian sky, about the horror lurking in the Marabar Caves and the release symbolized

by the birth of Krishna. It is - or rather desires to be   philosophic and poetic.

In the expression of philosophy and poetry Forster utilizes symbolic materials. He believes in an art which can give unity and pattern to experience. Indeed, he specifically praises the French novelist Proust for the inventiveness of the rhythmic phrase which works 'towards the establishment of beauty and the ravishing of the reader's memory' (*Aspects of the Novel*, p. 148). There is a discrepancy, in Forster's mind, between story, which is a primitive element running through a novel like 'a tapeworm' (*Aspects of the Novel*, p. 41), and the higher possibilities of the form. This discrepancy, between form and material, can only successfully be resolved through what he terms 'faking', a creative process which bestows organic form and order upon seemingly intractable material. An instance of this would be the organization of *A Passage to India* into three movements, 'Mosque', 'Caves' and 'Temple', sections which coincide not only with cool, hot and rainy seasons but also with Muslim, British and Hindu racial communities.

Forster places the reader in possession of these multiple viewpoints as a way of conveying the essence of Indian life. As he recorded in *The Hill of Devi*, 'everything that happens is said to be one thing and proves to be another'. In the Hindu universe as expounded by Professor Godbole, nothing is lost or insignificant and each layered segment of reality is inextricably woven into the continuum of time. A notable example of Forster's symbolic method in the novel is his employment of bee and wasp imagery. After the troublesome conversation with Ronny about her encounter in the mosque, Mrs Moore retires for the night, and as she does so she notices a wasp on a coat-peg. The insect sleeps, oblivious of the baying jackals and the drums which disturb the night air. In an act of love like that of the Ancient Mariner in Coleridge's poem, she blesses the insect, accepting its creaturely independence:

'Pretty dear,' said Mrs Moore to the wasp. He did not wake, but her voice floated out, to swell the night's uneasiness. (p. 55)

In the following chapter, the narrator turns to the well-meaning Christian missionaries and their ideal of brotherly love. Young Mr Sorley, who was 'advanced', wished to encompass not only different racial groups within the Christian embrace but also the animal kingdom of monkeys and jackals. Yet even he becomes uneasy 'during the descent to wasps, and was apt to change the conversation' (p. 58). The point is not underlined, but a profound distinction is registered between Mrs Moore's already Hinduistic pantheism and the exclusive categories of Western religion. Long after Mrs Moore's death, Professor Godbole enters into his mystical ecstasy at Mau under the heady influence of the musicians:

They loved all men, the whole universe, and scraps of their past, tiny splinters of detail, emerged for a moment to melt into the universal warmth. Thus Godbole, though she was not important to him, remembered an old woman he had met in Chandrapore days. Chance brought her into his mind while it was in this heated state, he did not select her, she happened to occur among the throng of soliciting images, a tiny splinter, and he impelled her by his spiritual force to that place where completeness can be found. Completeness, not reconstruction. His senses grew thinner, he remembered a wasp seen he forgot where, perhaps on a stone. He loved the wasp equally, he impelled it likewise, he was imitating God. And the stone where the wasp clung – could he ... no, he had been wrong to attempt the stone (pp. 283–4)

Although Godbole's thoughts proceed from within himself, he appears as part of a wider symbolic pattern in which he, Mrs Moore and the wasp are reunited. Forster bestows expression upon the material afforded by Godbole in its completeness of subjectivity. The old man does not simply meditate, but is presented as meditating and so is placed by the description. An ordering voice transforms the teeming chaos of impressions into a meaningful pattern. This act of pattern-making is reinforced a little later when Ralph Moore is stung by the bees at the shrine, since this incident finally draws Aziz and Mrs Moore's son together in compassionate alliance and enables the novel to circle back, now with the weight of its lived experience, to the opening encounter in the mosque. Ralph acts symbolically in another sense also: the repetition of Mrs Moore in the children of the second marriage emphasizes the distinction between Ronny Heaslop and his mother.

As with the bees and the wasps, so other features of the Indian landscape are utilized symbolically by the novelist. The most significant of these may be the echo which so affects Mrs Moore and Adela. The echoic effect does not emerge out of nowhere; rather is it carefully prepared by the narrative. At the Bridge Party, after Mrs Moore and Adela have attempted to 'connect' with the Bhatta-charyas, all genuine contact seems to dissipate itself against 'the echoing walls of their civility' (p. 62), just as Mrs Bhattacharya had 'echoed' the response of her husband (p. 63). Later that day, Mrs Moore reviews the situation:

> Mrs Moore felt that she had made a mistake in mentioning God, but she found Him increasingly difficult to avoid as she grew older, and He had been constantly in her thoughts since she entered India, though oddly enough He satisfied her less. She must needs pronounce His name frequently, as the greatest she knew, yet she had never found it less efficacious. Outside the arch there seemed always an arch, beyond the remotest echo a silence. (p. 71)

The novel increasingly stresses the function of sound as it moves towards its climax, and the sounds – Godbole's song, for instance, or the 'pomper, pomper, pomper' of the train wheels – imply repetition and vagueness of outline. It is this repetition and meaninglessness which explodes at the caves, whose echo reverberates throughout the rest of the book. Even after the partial clarification afforded by the trial, Fielding recognizes that the events of the caves can know no limits:

> 'In the old eighteenth century, when cruelty and injustice raged, an invisible power repaired their ravages. Everything echoes now; there's no stopping the echo. The original sound may be harmless, but the echo is always evil.' (p. 272)

Fielding has arrived here at a significant insight into human and natural relations, and the way they are continuously under threat. The echo effect resonates even to the conclusion, when Aziz, listening to the Hindu chant of 'Radhakrishna, Krishnaradha', hears 'in the interstice' 'the syllables of salvation that had sounded during his trial' – the chanting of 'Esmiss Esmoor' which had echoed outside the courtroom (p. 308).

Forster employs his symbols structurally, so that each section implies a meaning which is revised or modified by what comes after and before. In the first section the Muslim element dominates the action, but the caves are referred to with premonitory effect. In the third section the Hindu element is dominant. Mrs Moore's entry into the mosque at the outset gives her an instinctive comprehension of the Muslim way of life through her immediate personal understanding with Aziz. This understanding runs throughout the novel: Mrs Moore never doubts Aziz's innocence, and at the end Aziz confirms that Mrs Moore was his 'best friend'. The 'Mosque' section, therefore, stands in some sense for the 'secret understanding of the heart'. Before it ends, however, the caves have begun to

darken the horizon. At Fielding's tea-party, Godbole offers, then
fails, to describe them and this deliberate emphasis and absence
ominously foreshadows the next section of the book. The description of the hills and the caves demonstrates how the text is carrying
the characters beyond their own limits to a place where the secret
understanding of the heart is no longer adequate. The echo denies
all distinctions:

'Pathos, piety, courage – they exist, but are identical, and so is filth.
Everything exists, nothing has value.' If one had spoken vileness in that
place, or quoted lofty poetry, the comment would have been the same 'ou-
boum'. (p. 160)

After this no re-establishment is possible, and Mrs Moore dies.
Yet after her death she begins to act symbolically (as had Mrs
Wilcox in *Howards End*) in a redemptive capacity. The novel,
indeed, pairs her with Godbole in this role, and it is important to
note that even within the negative 'Caves' section it is Godbole who
expresses a wider and more reassuring interpretation of events at
the Marabar. Evil is simply the absence of good, and thus is
inextricably linked with it. God is still implored to come, as he was
in Godbole's song, and in the 'Temple' there is a sense in which
God arrives. In the Hindu ceremonials the violation of proportion
and decorum actually intensifies the spirituality of the participants,
and even of the English and Muslim outsiders. When Stella, in
one of the most profound symbolic gestures of the novel, leans
instinctively towards Aziz's boat, she causes the harmless sinking
of both boats in the shallow water. This unifying baptismal rite
occurs simultaneously with the cacophony of the Gokul Ashtami
ceremony and enacts a brief, but intensely felt, act of connection.
The function of these blocks of narrative is to create an effect in the
reader's mind akin to that of music, so that the structure possesses
something of the tripartite unity of sonata form, together with
a symbolic richness of suggestion which is particularly musical.
Forster's crucial observations in *Aspects of the Novel* about the
musical 'opening out' of the novel should be recalled once more.
What he says there of *War and Peace* is also applicable to his own
final novel:

Such an untidy book. Yet, as we read it, do not great chords begin to sound
behind us, and when we have finished does not every item ... lead a larger
existence than was possible at the time? (*Aspects of the Novel*, p. 150)

Some years after the composition of *A Passage to India*, Forster was to learn more about the architecture and iconography of the Hindu temple, which he dubbed 'The World Mountain'. On the outside of the temple, he observed, 'is displayed life in all its forms, life human and superhuman and subhuman and animal', while the interior consists of 'a tiny cavity, a central cell, where, in the heart of the world complexity, the individual could be alone with his god'. This description, though it post-dates the novel, is of some significance to the symbolism of the book. The world of European protestantism comes to seem, as the novel progresses, increasingly limited to those Europeans who seek contact. Whereas Christianity has been taken as an ethical code, the natural tendency of Hinduism is towards mystical unity, a striving for unity signified in the division of the book into tripartite objects and qualities: mosque, caves, temple; Muslim, British, Hindu; cool, hot, rainy; sky, earth, water, and so on. The unity possible upon a resolution of these divisions is partial and limited. As Godbole realizes in his mystical vision, identification with the absolute comes only with the extinction of individual will and the escape of the soul from the physical realm. The detachment and near invisibility of Godbole in the novel allow him a wider sense of proportion and detachment than can be achieved by other characters. The known world on the exterior of the world mountain, it might be argued, is represented by Fielding, Adela and Aziz, with their commitment to human relations and their unease at the realm of the unseen hinted at by Godbole, Mrs Moore and Stella. Forster's symbolism thus works to seek out and reinforce a sense of unity within the teeming multiplicity of Indian life; such a sense of unity is felt by the reader, but rarely by the characters.

In an interview for the *Paris Review* in 1952, Forster observed that as a novelist he required a 'sense of a solid mass ahead, a mountain round or over or through which the story must go'. He knew, he added, 'that something important happened in the Marabar Caves', but did not know 'what it would be'. Similarly, in bringing the novel to its conclusion, he felt that he needed 'a lump, or a Hindu temple'. These remarks can aid the reader to comprehend the imaginative power and function of Forster's symbols, their essentially unwilled and spontaneous nature. The meaning of the novel is enacted through the descriptions perhaps to a larger extent than in Forster's earlier works where nature acts as a moral contrast to the characters. The landscapes of India may not be truly comprehensible, but this sense of incomprehensibility is communicated through the pattern of symbols which at least hints at possibilities of comprehension.

Adela's crisis at the heart of the novel is symbolic of a wider breakdown of sympathy and connection between the two races. She has sought to know the 'real' India, just as Mrs Moore has sought to love it. The events at the caves suggest that the 'passage' of the title is impossible of realization, despite the emphasis the novelist places upon the motif of the invitation. Each invitation in the novel fails in its intentions: the Bridge Party, Fielding's tea-party, the missionaries' encompassing love of all creative life, the Marabar picnic, all dissolve into muddle and incoherence within a landscape which, the narrator remarks, 'tries to keep men in compartments' (p. 141). The threat of this landscape, its corrosive effect upon human relations, is distilled and enacted in the caves, the central enigmatic symbol of *A Passage to India*.

In seeking to unravel the enigma it is useful to glance first at some likely source material. In Kipling's travel book, *From Sea to Sea* (1900), there is a passage describing some Indian caves:

from the Gau-Mukh, a passage led to the subterranean chambers ... some sort of devil, or ghoul, or something, stood at the entrance of that approach ... not exactly a feeling of danger or pain, but an apprehension of great evil.

If this served to suggest the emanation of evil at the Marabar, a sequence in Richard Jefferies' *The Story of my Heart* (1883) may lie behind the terrifying echo. The 'spiritual autobiography' of this nature mystic was referred to by Leonard Bast in *Howards End*, and it seems likely that Forster knew it well. In the sixth chapter, Jefferies, contemplating the roar of the London traffic, imagines himself back on the Wiltshire downs in summer: 'Burning in the sky, the sun shone on me', he recalls, 'as when I rested in the narrow valley carved in prehistoric time.' Reviewing past cultures, Jefferies goes on:

The aged caves of India, who shall tell when they were sculptured? Far back when the sun was burning, burning in the sky as now in untold precedent time. Is there any meaning in those ancient caves? The indistinguishable noise not to be resolved, born of the human struggle, mocks in answer.

This roar 'is not resolvable', and 'no attention can resolve it into a fixed sound', just as the Marabar echo is 'entirely devoid of distinction' (pp. 158–9). The indistinguishable noise, in Jefferies' mind, 'roars a loud contempt', a contempt perhaps reflected in the message of Forster's caves that ' "Everything exists, nothing has value" ' (p. 160). Yet there is a positive force embodied in Jefferies' vision; beyond the roar, he observes:

> I feel the presence of the sun, of the immense forces of the universe, and beyond these the sense of the eternal now, of the immortal

Sun worship opens the way, in Jefferies, to a mystically apprehended 'soul-life'. By contrast, the sun in India returns to his kingdom 'with power but without beauty': 'Through excess of light, he failed to triumph' and is 'debarred from glory' (p. 127). Yet the soul-life which transcends the meaningless roar for Jefferies may in some respects point forward to Godbole's mystical vision of unity. If Kipling and Jefferies are present at a subtextual level, the sense of that presence can aid the reader towards a definition of the meaning of the caves.

It is in the caves that the colonial visitors meet a critical point. The picnic at the Marabar is envisaged as uniting Muslim, Christian and Hindu. The hills are 'older than all spirit', and go back long before Hinduism 'scratched and plastered a few rocks' (p. 137). They are removed from man and history, and 'Nothing, nothing attaches to them' (p. 138). This nihilism annihilates value for Mrs Moore, and in the caves she enters 'the twilight of the double vision' through her encounter with something 'snub-nosed, incapable of generosity' (p. 212). Seeing through the world of appearance, she is left with no sense of reality. She would like to be 'one with the universe' (p. 212), in the sense desiderated by the Romantic poets, but the oneness she attains, in its monotony and apathy, is wholly destructive. All categories and differentiations are swallowed up in the 'boum' of the echo, an effect which 'robbed infinity and eternity of their vastness, the only quality that accommodates them to mankind' (p. 161). Mrs Moore's thoughts, distorted by the caves, are of religion; Adela's, on the other hand, are sexual. Approaching the second cave with Aziz, her mind is full of misgivings about her marriage to Ronny, and she recognizes that she is not in love. She determines to suppress this lack, and to proceed with the marriage. She observes Aziz's sexual attractiveness and commits the blunder of asking him how many wives he has. The imagined attack issues out of this complex tissue of repressed sexual feeling, and it is not until she can abandon her Westernized reliance upon causality as explanation that she can retract her charge: there is a form of truth beyond her rationalism. In a physical sense, it would seem that nothing has happened to her. But that nothingness exerts a frightening pressure as a form of ultimate negation which is expressed as an attempted rape. The repeated 'ou-boum', it may be, is an expression of the unconscious which Adela has ruthlessly repressed, an unconscious which now takes over her mind with terrifying effect: 'the echo flourished, raging up and down like a nerve in the faculty of her hearing, and the noise in the cave, so unimportant intellectually, was prolonged over the surface of her life' (p. 200). Adela is alienated from her feelings, and the echo precipitates a profound inner crisis, an inability to accept her own shadow self, double or opposite, the emanation of her own subconscious.

The narrative remarks of the caves, 'Nothing, nothing attaches to them, and their reputation ... does not depend upon human speech' (p. 138). The concepts of nothingness and absence of speech are both crucial to an understanding of the caves' significance. They are, essentially, an absence in the text, a gap or hole which affects the presence of the rest of the book. Their effect may be compared to the way in which the *avant-garde* French novelist Alain Robbe-Grillet described the structure of his novel, *Le Voyeur*:

> Everything is told before 'the hole', then again after 'the hole', and there is an effort to bring together the two edges to eliminate this troublesome emptiness; but the opposite occurs, 'the hole' engulfs everything.

One principal effect of the 'troublesome emptiness' of the caves is to undermine linguistic difference, the difference upon which creation of meaning depends. All human speech is here reduced to 'boum'. If several people begin to speak, 'at once an overlapping howling noise begins' (p. 159). This engulfing sound threatens the rational discourse upon which Western power is based and through which it is expressed, for example, in the National Anthem:

> It was the Anthem of the Army of Occupation. It reminded every member of the Club that he or she was British and in exile. It produced a little sentiment and a useful accession of will-power. The meagre tune, the curt series of demands on Jehovah, fused into a prayer unknown in England. (p. 47)

Instead of a clearly articulated system of language in which it is assumed that words have an agreed referential function, the caves produce a babel of sound which reduplicates the enigma of the 'snake' which may be a rope on a larger scale. The normative concept of the relation between language and reality is dizzyingly undermined, and definable meaning blotted out or postponed.

The words spoken in the caves are subject to a kind of self-deconstruction. Language as a signifying system is appropriated by a dominant group, in this case the colonial power, but the caves, in their riddling complexity, dismantle the slogans of the dominant culture. The culture evinced at the Club and in the Civil Station at large is unmistakably male and patriarchal, and it may be no accident that the characters who expose themselves to the caves should both be female. In the din of the caves Mrs Moore realizes that all the words of her religion 'only amounted to "boum"' (p. 161). The disappearance of the central female characters into the caves, and the undecipherability of the events within them, radically unsettle the narrative action to produce a blur and an absence at the point of crisis. To Lowes Dickinson's inquiry, 'What did happen in the caves?', Forster replied, 'My writing mind is a blur here – i.e. I will it to remain a blur'. He went on to refer to his technique at this point as 'voluntary surrender to infection'. It has been claimed that there is the 'wound of a fracture that lies hidden in all texts', and certainly the caves take the form of a fracture in the solid structure of *A Passage to India*. The 'inner meaning' of the text, in this view, may be nothing other than its external features infolded to create an inner space which is both secret and empty, just as the 'World Mountain' of the Hindu temple contains within itself its own opposite.

Entry into the caves is a return to the womb and to a pre-verbal existence. Language is a symbolic system through which power is exerted, but this power is radically challenged by what happens at the Marabar: ' "Pathos, piety, courage – they exist, but are identical, and so is filth. Everything exists, nothing has value"' (p. 160). The puzzle of the caves may be illuminated by some reference to the theory of language propounded by George Steiner in his essay, 'The Language Animal'.* Steiner argues that authoritarian models of society lay claim to the inner identity of the human person through deformation of language, of the kind registered by the tribal hysteria of the scenes at the Club. The ruling class, here the colonizers, exert power through an 'artifice of unanimous memory' which 'replaces the natural plurality of the individual recall'. In such a society, the multiple realities of India will be blotted out as Steiner indicates:

To unspeak the actual past, to eradicate the names, arts, thoughts of the uncounted dead, is a tyranny of peculiar horror. Pursued rigorously, it cuts

* In *Extraterritorial* (Penguin, 1975), pp. 66–109.

off humanity, or certain societies, from the vital responsibilities of mourning and of justice. Man is set back in a landscape without echo.

The echo thus suppressed through the imposition of colonial authority, with its deliberate 'forgetting' of India's culture, religions and history, returns with a vengeance in the Marabar. Modern linguistic inquiry suggests that language underlies and perpetuates human patterns of behaviour, and that the very question of identity, of 'I' and 'you', is predicated upon and created through language. The process of a statement from a self and response by a non-self is dialectical, and the breakdown in this dialectic is registered in some strange remarks of Mrs Moore's:

'Why all this marriage, marriage? ... The human race would have become a single person centuries ago if marriage was any use. And all this rubbish about love, love in a church, love in a cave, as if there is the least difference . . .' (p. 207)

The origins of the individual's humanity lie in the evolution of language, and it is back towards pre-linguistic origins that Mrs Moore and Adela are compelled to penetrate. Speech, as Steiner explains, never really ceases in the human being: 'Even when we are outwardly mute, speech is active within and our skull is like an echo chamber.' The caves, in this sense, are the retreat into the deepest reverberating recesses of the psyche, recesses where our Western habits of cognition and perception are ineffectual. Steiner argues that language function is part of our creativity. The exercise of human language, he asserts, 'enacts, albeit on a microscopically humble scale, the divine reflex of creation, the *logos* or "speaking into being" of the universe'. This creative act is demolished in the caves, where all the 'divine words' of 'poor little talkative Christianity' 'only amounted to "boum"' (p. 161).

The production of a babel of sound might be related to Steiner's thesis of a linguistic crisis which, beginning in the early twentieth century, both reflects and enables the political and moral disintegration of the order of liberal humanism in Europe and beyond. Where definitions break down, Steiner observes, 'where syntax dissolves, the old chaos returns, either in the pathology of an individual or in the collapse of a society'. The narrative of *A Passage to India* examines both: individual pathology in Mrs Moore and Adela, and portents of breakdown in British rule in India. In the case of Adela it is significant that the narrative blocks the central heterosexual relationship so as to sustain the emphasis upon the Fielding–Aziz connection. While Forster's own sexual nature is carefully muffled in the novel, one of Steiner's queries casts a riddling light upon underlying tendencies: 'May one raise the question', he demands, 'of a possible relation between homosexuality and certain theories of language as a game, as a complex of internalized conventions and mirrorings?' The mirror effect of the polished walls of the caves serves as an emblem of the blocking of 'normal' relations in the novel: 'The two flames approach and strive to unite, but cannot, because one of them breathes air, the other stone' (p. 138). Seeking the sources of language, Steiner notes, 'may be a circular process, a juggling with mirrors', and that circularity is enacted in the novel, where like seeks like, the self seeks the mirror image of itself rather than its opposite, and Adela and Mrs Moore are brought face to face with a primal lawless realm of instinct, bewilderingly self-propagating, non-verbal and dreamlike. This is a reality which their waking lives have been devoted to repressing; more widely, it is a reality which the dominant patriarchy of colonialism seeks to blot out and deny. The child, Freud argued, begins to formulate the concept of self by seeing his or her reflection in the mirror. What happens to Adela and Mrs Moore is a symbolic reversal of the formation of the self through language and socialization, an immersion into the endlessly reduplicating mirrors and echoes of the caves. Individual selfhood, the bedrock of Western thought, is exposed here in all its bankruptcy. After the symbolic descent into the caves, the novel can move onwards towards the healing unity of the Hindu temple.

The Marabar Caves stand as the major symbolic episode of the novel. During the plunge into the caves the temporal momentum of the narrative is suspended, the forward-moving plot dislocated by the potent simultaneity of metaphoric creation. But the novel, however reluctantly, tells a story, and Adela's painful descent to Miss Derek's car allows that story to resume and develop, achieving its more conventional realist crisis in the trial scene.

Through parallel and repetition the central symbol of the novel, the cave, is carefully linked into the entire narrative pattern. Indeed, the act of entry into the Marabar will, however unconsciously, remind the reader of Aziz's entry into the mosque:

The covered part of the mosque was deeper than is usual; its effect was that of an English parish church whose side has been taken out. Where he sat, he looked into three arcades whose darkness was illuminated by a small hanging lamp and by the moon. The front – in full moonlight – had the appearance of marble, and the ninety-nine names of God on the frieze stood out black, as the frieze stood out white against the sky. (p. 41)

The order of beauty and proportion here, to which the arrival of Mrs Moore bears witness, is to be subverted and reversed by the suffocating darkness and emptiness of the caves. This nullity is in its turn balanced by the final sacred building, the Hindu courtyard at Mau, characterized as a joyous mass of chaos:

It was of beautiful hard white stucco, but its pillars and vaulting could scarcely be seen behind coloured rags, iridescent balls, chandeliers of opaque pink glass, and murky photographs framed crookedly. At the end was the small but famous shrine of the dynastic cult, and the God to be born was largely a silver image the size of a teaspoon. Hindus sat on either side of the carpet where they could find room, or overflowed into the adjoining corridors and the courtyard. (p. 281)

The implications of each successive interior are worked out in the structure of the novel, and the unifying and divisive tendencies scrupulously balanced so as to produce the beautifully subdued symbolism of the final ride of Fielding and Aziz:

They cantered past a temple to Hanuman – God so loved the world that he took monkey's flesh upon him – and past a Saivite temple, which invited to lust, but under the semblance of eternity, its obscenities bearing no relation to those of our flesh and blood. They splashed through butterflies and frogs; great trees with leaves like plates rose among the brushwood. The divisions of daily life were returning, the shrine had almost shut. (p. 315)

Through the marshalling of the large symbols of mosque, caves and temple, and the related deployment of interdependent motifs – snake, wasp, sun and moon – *A Passage to India* achieves a symbolic order which, however temporary, transcends the warring multiplicities of reality in a sustained act of creative 'faking'.

Comedy and irony

A Passage to India is not a novel one would immediately describe as 'comic'. It does not keep us constantly, or even intermittently, amused. However, it *is* difficult to decide how to describe the effect of the novel, and one of the reader's impressions is likely to be that it is witty and urbane in tone. The pervasive presence of an authorial voice, and its commentating role, convey a certain attitude towards the characters and events of the novel, an attitude that is often critical of social mores, detached and incisive. Forster frequently uses dialogue to highlight comic misunderstandings and to attack pretensions and prejudices. As in Jane Austen's novels the dramatic irony implicit in many interactions and in a more general development of events is controlled and exhibited by a writer who adopts a prominent position between the reader and the characters.

In his earlier novels, Forster takes a critical stance towards the English middle classes, showing their lack of imagination, intolerance, snobbishness and materialism. Foreign cultures in *Where Angels Fear to Tread* and *A Room with a View*, nuances of class distinction in, for example, *The Longest Journey* and *Howards End*, a different kind of sexuality in *Maurice*: all are posed as threats or challenges to the middle class, and their tendency to react by withdrawal, dismissal or contempt is revealed. It is frequently observed by critics that this satirical treatment of the middle classes is historically located in the Edwardian era, years when they were apparently secure and complacent. The developing tensions and insecurities of this stratum of society after the Great War, and the changed nature of the economic, social and political landscapes, posed some dilemmas for Forster. The middle class was no longer a citadel which deserved to be stormed, but rather became part of an era to be regarded nostalgically, and the ironic domestic comedy in Forster's work lost some of its immediate relevance. Literature was changing in theme and technique, too, and Forster's readership was also encountering uncompromisingly post-war works like *The Waste Land* and *Women in Love*. These dilemmas may be discerned in *A Passage to India*. The difficulties caused by the novel's debt to two visits to India so widely apart in time have already been touched upon. It often seems that Forster's depiction of the intolerance of the Anglo-Indian community derives from his pre-war encounters with them, while much of the general mood of the novel, for example, the nihilistic vision in the caves, is post-war in sensibility and emphasis.

These historical difficulties can, however, be over-stressed. Forster posed himself another challenge: to portray Indians in a way that recognized racial characteristics and quirks, but that avoided prejudiced stereotyping, condescension, or collusion with a readership who might be tempted to identify their sympathies with Anglo-Indians. In fact, at another level, Forster does not avoid categorizing Indians in terms of certain received notions of racial difference: we may dissent from his very assumption that Indians are on the whole volatile, unreliable, dreamy and emotional. He displays as truths what are sometimes ideologically questionable notions, such as when he says, of Adela and Aziz, 'She did not admire him with any personal warmth, for there was nothing of the vagrant in her blood' (p. 163). Here, despite a possible irony, Forster seems to assume that sexual attraction between the races implies 'vagrancy' within the (white, female) temperament. However, Forster himself perceived his problem as being one of balance, and of how to avoid replicating prejudices about Indians in his portrayal of them. The result, in *A Passage to India*, produced several indignant complaints that he had distorted the Anglo-Indians to an unforgivable extent. Not only were they 'inhuman' and 'preposterous', but the comparison with the Indian characters was unflattering to the Anglo-Indian characters. It is difficult at this point to distinguish between complaints about the element of caricature in the Anglo-Indians (a technical and aesthetic criticism), and complaints that the Indians had been treated more sympathetically at the expense of the Anglo-Indians (a criticism of Forster's sympathies, rooted in some degree of racial prejudice). Forster cheerfully admitted that his sympathies lay with Indians: 'I don't like Anglo-Indians as a class. I tried to suppress this and be fair to them, but my lack of sympathy came through.' He went on to reject a charge that he had been irresponsible, arguing that balance in such a situation of racial tension proves to be impossible:

> You say I don't like them because I don't really know them. But how can I ever like them when I happen to like the Indians and they don't? They don't (this part of my picture you do not challenge) – so what am I to do? Sympathy is finite – at least mine is, alas, – so that as the rope is pulled into the right hand it slips out of the left. If I saw more of Anglo-India at work (or shared its work, which is the only sympathetic seeing) I should of course realize its difficulties and loyalties better and write about it from within. Well and good, but you forget the price to be paid: I should begin to write about Indians from without. My statements about them might be the same, but the accent would have altered.

A Passage to India, however, does not 'side' with the Indians to the extent that it portrays the Indians solemnly and Anglo-Indians satirically. Forster is characteristically a detached and ironic novelist, and all the characters are at one point or another viewed with humour or irony. What does happen is that there is a tendency to satirize the Anglo-Indians and to portray the Indians with a more genial fondness. John Colmer, for example, makes the point that

'The novelist takes care that the mistakes of such sympathetic characters as Aziz and the Nawab are either endearing or innocently comic'.

It is difficult to laugh at a character without introducing an element of condescension into one's attitude. The presentation of Godbole is particularly interesting in this respect. Forster attempts to invite us to laugh at the vagueness and impracticality of Godbole in such matters as his miscalculation of the length of his prayers on the day of the excursion to the caves, and to regard his affliction with piles as amusingly undignified. Yet he is introduced as an emblem of harmony: 'as if he had reconciled the products of East and West, mental as well as physical, and could never be discomposed' (p. 89). His song is moving and thematically central to the novel, and in his religious ecstasy at the end of the novel there is a combination of humorous presentation with serious authorial intention. The enigma of Professor Godbole, and of how we are to read his role and presence in the novel, is never solved. Indeed, many critics interpret the enigma as being the point – that Forster shows muddle and mystery, comedy and poetry, existing in inextricable connection. Beyond this interpretive process, though, there remains the problem of presenting in a comic light a character of another race, deemed 'inferior' in the historical context of the novel's production and composition.

A closer consideration of Forster's techniques and effects will be useful here. When Godbole visits Fielding after Aziz's arrest, he eventually asks, with a comically inappropriate interest in the excursion, about what they saw:

And he related a legend which might have been acceptable if he had told it at the tea-party a fortnight ago. It concerned a Hindu rajah who had slain his own sister's son, and the dagger with which he performed the deed remained clamped to his hand until in the course of years he came to the Marabar Hills, where he was thirsty and wanted to drink but saw a thirsty cow and ordered the water to be offered to her first, which, when done, 'dagger fell from his hand, and to commemorate miracle he built Tank'. Professor Godbole's conversations frequently culminated in a cow. Fielding received this one in gloomy silence. (pp. 186–7)

The passage shows great control in comic timing, through the pace and length of sentences. The synopsis of Godbole's story is given in one sentence, which becomes progressively more shorthand, as if to convey the tedium of the predictable plot, and an auditor's exasperation. The sentence also highlights the disjunction between East and West, here between the Eastern storyteller and the Western auditor, a disjunction which is reinforced in the following sentence, where the authorial voice adopts an urbane view of Eastern preoccupations: the monosyllable of 'cow' at the end of the sentence creates an effect of bathos. Fielding's reaction of 'gloomy silence' has already been prepared for by the enactment of Godbole's long-winded tale. A broader comic effect is also achieved by the observation that the story is unacceptable in these circumstances, but would have thrilled Adela and Mrs Moore at Fielding's tea-party, when Godbole refused to say anything about the caves. Godbole's disregard for social appropriateness is exasperating.

Another example of Forster's comic timing occurs during Fielding's tea-party. When Adela and Mrs Moore ask Aziz why the Bhattacharyas failed to send their carriage for them, Aziz condemns them as being 'slack Hindus'. Within seconds he has impulsively invited the Englishwomen to his home, but when Adela asks him for his address,

Aziz thought of his bungalow with horror. It was a detestable shanty near a low bazaar. There was practically only one room in it, and that infested with small black flies. 'Oh, but we will talk of something else now,' he exclaimed. (pp. 86–7)

The comedy here arises from the difference between Aziz's intentions and his willingness to carry them out. He has just condemned Hindus for the very 'slackness' which he is guilty of, and ironically, the failed invitation of the Bhattacharyas leads indirectly to his invitation, which is just as impracticable.

Timing and a variety of different social and racial idioms provide a comic effect when Miss Derek rescues Ronny, Adela and the Nawab after their car accident. The Nawab, upset and disconcerted, launches into a speech about Indian superstition:

He grew more and more voluble. 'Oh, it is the duty of each and every citizen to shake superstition off, and though I have little experience of Hindu States, and none of this particular one, namely Mudkul (the Ruler, I fancy, has a salute of but eleven guns) – yet I cannot imagine that they have been as successful as British India, where we see reason and orderliness spreading in every direction, like a most health-giving flood!'
Miss Derek said 'Golly!' (pp. 107–8)

The Nawab, who obviously knows nothing about Mudkul, nevertheless passes judgement, and is drawn into a florid and extravagant tribute to the British. His tendency to inflate his vocabulary is followed by the English expletive, 'Golly!' (Far later in the novel, his praise for British 'reason and orderliness' is ironically disproved by their response to Adela's accusation of Aziz.) The authorial voice refers to the Nawab as 'this old geyser', reflecting the reaction of the three young English people, but they all refrain from commenting on his performance: 'Ronny made no comment, but talked lightly about polo; Turton had taught him that it is sounder not to discuss a man at once, and he reserved what he had to say on the Nawab's character until later in the evening' (p. 108). Furthermore, the Nawab's condemnation of superstition is later to be followed by the revelation that the Nawab himself is extremely superstitious about what the car might have collided with.

As well as providing comedy through dialogue and cultural differences, Forster creates ironic effects through echoes and references to previous incidents, which the alert reader is expected to notice. Thus the collar-stud, which is so indicative of Aziz's impulsiveness and generosity, and which comes to stand for the developing relationship between Aziz and Fielding, is noted and interpreted very differently by Ronny: ' "he had forgotten his back collar-stud, and there you have the Indian all over: inattention to detail; the fundamental slackness that reveals the race" ' (p. 97). The tragedy of the British inability to understand the Indian psyche is hinted at here. Another example is the subaltern's memory of playing polo with an Indian on the Maidan, which he illogically mentions during the crisis meeting at the Club after Aziz's arrest. The reader, and Forster, are in the position to know that he is in fact referring to Aziz, whom the British are presently condemning.

It is worth noting that in all these examples Forster suggests some degree of sympathy with the Indian side of the relationship. Aziz, in particular, is portrayed as lovable and victimized by these misunderstandings and ironies. As the novel progresses, and as Aziz's unfortunate experiences culminate in his arrest and imprisonment, the comic incidents diminish: the misunderstandings have been seen to lead to serious results. John Beer makes a more general point about the tendency of Forster's comedy to develop into seriousness and emotional commitment, when he says:

> The reader who comes to Forster looking for social comedy ... will ... meet with disappointments. He will be put out by the fact that the novels are not only serious in basic intention but sometimes deliberately flat in their immediate effect.

And Forster himself, in an interview in 1952, admitted that he learned from Jane Austen 'the possibilities of domestic humour. I was more ambitious than she was, of course; I tried to hitch it on to other things.'

There are, then, problems associated with attempting to describe Forster as a 'comic' novelist in this sense. However, throughout his novels, Forster has been interested in, and has celebrated, a spirit of abandon, disorder and wholeness which expresses and enriches the individual. The festival of Gokul Ashtami epitomizes the combination of deep feeling and human idiosyncrasy that Forster finds so attractive, and in itself this might be termed a 'comic spirit'. Forster was attracted to Hinduism partly because he felt that it allows for humour; in *A Passage to India*, he says,

There is fun in heaven. God can play practical jokes upon Himself, draw chairs away from beneath His own posteriors, set His own turbans on fire, and steal His own petticoats when He bathes. By sacrificing good taste, this worship achieved what Christianity has shirked: the inclusion of merriment. (p. 286)

The examples of practical jokes here – and Forster himself was subjected to exploding cigarettes and whisky-and-salt on April Fool's Day 1921 at the Rajah's court – are less important than the spirit of freedom that they express. In technical terms, this 'comic spirit' is displayed in Forster's fiction in a Meredithian way. Forster was greatly influenced by the works of George Meredith (1828–1909), who besides writing a number of novels, also produced a widely read essay on comedy and the comic spirit. Forster discusses Meredith's fiction in *Aspects of the Novel*:

A Meredithian plot is not a temple to the tragic or even to the comic Muse, but rather resembles a series of kiosks most artfully placed among wooded slopes, which his people reach by their own impetus, and from which they emerge with altered aspect. Incident springs out of character, and having occurred it alters that character. People and events are closely connected, and he does it by means of these contrivances. They are often delightful, sometimes touching, always unexpected. (p. 90)

The close connection between character and event, the elements of contrivance and the unexpected: these are also evident in Forster's fiction, and they express his liking for a general mood of lively spontaneity. The 'comic spirit' is present when Aziz, Fielding, Stella and Ralph capsize into the lake at the climax of the religious festivities, so that

The oars, the sacred tray, the letters of Ronny and Adela, broke loose and floated confusedly. Artillery was fired, drums beaten, the elephants trumpeted, and drowning all an immense peal of thunder, unaccompanied by lightning, cracked like a mallet on the dome.

That was the climax, as far as India admits of one. (p. 310)

The colonial encounter

In the first place, I believe in the British Empire and, in the second place, I believe in the British race. I believe that the British race is the greatest of governing races that the world has ever seen.

Joseph Chamberlain

We are the first race in the world, and, the more of the world we inhabit, the better it is for the human race.

Cecil Rhodes

At the time of its publication in 1924, and for some time afterwards, *A Passage to India* was read primarily as a political novel which had made a significant and controversial contribution to the debates about the government of India. Forster said of the book, 'It had some political influence – it caused people to think of the link between India and Britain and to doubt if that link was altogether of a healthy nature'. Recent analysis of the novel has tended to place the emphasis elsewhere. In stressing the symbolic and poetic qualities of the novel, the social and political questions it raises have been subsumed. John Colmer, for instance, identifies the central question of the novel as that of 'men's relation to God, or of men's trying to understand each other and the universe'. Wilfred Stone, in the course of his Jungian interpretation, remarks that 'one of the aims of the book is to make people and their politics look small'. This strategy is one which defuses the political ambiguity of the text. Forster affirmed after Independence that 'the political side' was 'an aspect I wanted to express', and it is often this aspect which a critical idealism, in foregrounding mythic and symbolic elements, suppresses. For all its larger gestures *A Passage to India* is grounded in time and place with considerable exactitude. Its action is explicable only within that context, however the narrator widens and universalizes the experiences which are dramatized for the reader.

Indeed, the novel touches upon a number of real persons and events relating to the period. It is well known, for instance, that

Aziz is partly based upon Forster's close friend, Syed Ross Masood. Fielding, while possessing a good deal of the author's own philosophy, probably reflects the experience of his friend Malcolm Darling. Darling, a colonial administrator in India at the time of the Amritsar massacre, found himself ostracized by his Club for criticizing Dyer's action. Perhaps most interestingly, the plight of Adela Quested shows marked similarities with the case of Marcella Sherwood. Miss Sherwood was attacked by a mob during the riots at Amritsar, an incident which led Dyer to issue his so-called 'crawling order' that any Indian wishing to go down the street where the Englishwoman was attacked should do so on hands and knees. The order is clearly echoed in Mrs Turton's outburst at the Club: ' "Why, they ought to crawl from here to the caves on their hands and knees whenever an Englishwoman's in sight..." ' (p. 220). Despite the uprising, Marcella Sherwood refused compensation, and wrote to *The Times* asserting that her survival was thanks to the courage of her Indian pupils. She also described how Hindus and Muslims had united to prevent an attack on a hospital similar to the one in the novel averted by the antics of Dr Panna Lal. By working such events into the texture of the novel, Forster placed it with great deliberation within the ferment of nationalist debate and activity.

Forster once described himself as 'an individualist and a liberal who has found liberalism crumbling beneath him and at first felt ashamed. Then, looking around, he decided there was no special reason for shame, since other people, whatever they felt, were equally insecure. And as for individualism – there seems no way of getting off this, even if one wanted to' ('What I Believe', 1939, *Two Cheers for Democracy*, pp. 83–4). The enormous historical impulse of colonization and empire building during the nineteenth century placed liberals in an awkward and ambivalent position, an ambivalence neatly registered by the founding, in 1903, of *The Independent Review*, which Forster said was published 'to combat the aggressive Imperialism and the Protection Campaign of Joe Chamberlain; and to advocate sanity in foreign affairs and a constructive policy at home'. The liberal conscience, while not opposed to Empire, distrusted its jingoistic side. The dilemma of the thoughtful European had been scrupulously examined by Joseph Conrad, notably in *Heart of Darkness* (1902), and it was a problem which Forster had already addressed in his earlier fiction. In *Howards End*, published in 1910, the heroine Margaret Schlegel has reason to visit the offices of the Imperial and West African Rubber Company, where her fiancé Henry Wilcox holds sway:

There was just the ordinary surface scum of ledgers and polished counters and brass bars that began and stopped for no possible reason, of electric-light globes blossoming in triplets, of little rabbit-hutches faced with glass or wire, of little rabbits. And even when she penetrated to the inner depths, she found only the ordinary table and Turkey carpet, and though the map over the fireplace did depict a helping of West Africa, it was a very ordinary map. Another map hung opposite, on which the whole continent appeared, looking like a whale marked out for blubber, and by its side was a door ... perhaps she was seeing the Imperial side of the company rather than its West African, and Imperialism always had been one of her difficulties. (*Howards End*, p. 183)

This is a powerfully emblematic passage: its description of Westernized order, decorum and money in the 'polished counters and brass bars' is held against a mysterious sense of 'inner depths', and the simile of the whale epitomizes the desecration going on throughout the continent in the name of progress. Margaret, a typical product of Bloomsbury, finds imperialism 'one of her difficulties', just as her creator was to do two years later on his first visit to India. In his book *Gora*, published in the same year as *A Passage to India*, the poet Rabindranath Tagore invited Westerners to approach the sub-continent in terms exactly applicable to Forster's project:

Come inside India, accept all her good and evil: if there be deformity then try and cure it from within; but see it with your own eyes, understand it, think it over, turn your face towards it, become one with it.

The liberal-humanist approach to the government of the sub-continent was one which cut right across received notions in the literary treatment of the subject. For the British audience at home, the image of India had largely been created by Rudyard Kipling. In such stories as 'Stalky and Co.', 'At the End of the Passage', 'The Last Relief' and 'William the Conqueror', Kipling portrayed the colonial service as one imbued with the public school values of discipline and dedication in their dealings with what he termed, in his poem, 'Recessional', 'lesser breeds without the law'. Describing a raging epidemic in 'The Last Relief', Kipling remarks how 'The chain of men parted for an instant at the stroke [of death], but it closed up again, and continued to drag the empire forward, and not one living link of it rang false or was weak'. This Kiplingesque voice finds its expression in the Chandrapore Club. After Aziz's arrest, for instance, McBryde tells Fielding, '"at a time like this there's no room for – well – personal views. The man who doesn't toe the line is lost ... If you leave the line, you leave a gap in the line"' (p. 180). Ronny Heaslop's religion 'was of the sterilized public-school brand, which never goes bad, even in the tropics. Wherever he entered, mosque, cave or temple, he retained the spiritual outlook of the Fifth Form' (p. 256). Forster believed in approaching the Indian experience openly, and argued that 'You cannot understand the modern Indians unless you realize that politics occupy them passionately and constantly'. *A Passage to India*, by dramatizing Indian aspirations, directly confronted the image of India formulated by Kipling and his imitators. This dramatization often takes the form of an exploration of the difficulties of communication between the communities of rulers and ruled. As the Bridge Party draws to its close, for example, the dialogue neatly registers disturbance and misunderstanding: Mrs Moore asks if she might visit Mrs Bhattacharya:

'When?' she replied, inclining charmingly.

'Whenever is convenient.'

'All days are convenient.'

'Thursday ...'

'Most certainly.'

'We shall enjoy it greatly, it would be a real pleasure. What about the time?'

'All hours.'

'Tell us which you would prefer. We're quite strangers to your country; we don't know when you have visitors,' said Miss Quested.

Mrs Bhattacharya seemed not to know either. Her gesture implied that she had known, since Thursdays began, that English ladies would come to see her on one of them, and so always stayed in. Everything pleased her, nothing surprised. She added, 'We leave for Calcutta today.'

'Oh, do you?' said Adela, not at first seeing the implication. Then she cried, 'Oh, but if you do we shall find you gone.'

Mrs Bhattacharya did not dispute it. But her husband called from the distance, 'Yes, yes, you come to us Thursday.'

'But you'll be in Calcutta.'

'No, no, we shall not.' He said something swiftly to his wife in Bengali. 'We expect you Thursday.'

'Thursday ...' the woman echoed. (p. 63)

The verbal and philosophical confusions here about time and place, and the foretaste of the echoing multiplicity of the caves, help to reflect differences in attitude to reality and time between an industrialized state and a developing country. The text displays two different kinds of speech to enact the gulf which yawns between the groups. Similarly, when Fielding expresses doubts about the existence of God at Aziz's house, 'The Indians were bewildered. The line of thought was not alien to them, but the words were too definite and bleak' (pp. 124–5). However, the novel goes beyond this in exploring the fissures within each camp. When Godbole's illness is reported, suspicions are immediately aroused:

'If this is so, this is a very serious thing; this is scarcely the end of March. Why have I not been informed?' cried Aziz.

'Dr Panna Lal attends him, sir.'

'Oh yes, both Hindus; there we have it; they hang together like flies and keep everything dark.'   (pp. 117–18)

Life in India, it would seem, demands a dualistic sense of reality. Thus it is that many of the events in the novel take on different meanings from differing perspectives. When Major Callendar calls out Aziz, he blames his Indian subordinate for failing to turn up, whereas the reader knows the efforts Aziz has made to answer the call. When Mrs Moore describes her encounter with Aziz in the mosque, her feelings of warmth and friendship are directly contradicted by Ronny's misreading of the incident. When the Nawab's car is involved in a collision, the language aptly mirrors underlying racial distinctions and interpretative habits: the young people seek to detect a palpable cause, tracing back 'the writhing of the tyres to the source of their disturbance' (p. 104); Mrs Moore, when told of the incident, mutters the word 'ghost', and this is endorsed by the Nawab's secret memory of a man he had run over near this spot nine years earlier. The narrative layering seems to multiply outwards into confusions of appearance and reality, shadow and substance. Such confusions come to a head in the sight of the 'snake' on the way to the Marabar Caves:

Miss Quested saw a thin, dark object reared on end at the further side of a water-course, and said, 'A snake!' The villagers agreed, and Aziz explained: yes, a black cobra, very venomous, who had reared himself up to watch the passing of the elephant. But when she looked through Ronny's field-glasses she found it wasn't a snake, but the withered and twisted stump of a toddy-palm. So she said, 'It isn't a snake.' The villagers contradicted her. She had put the word into their minds, and they refused to abandon it. (p. 152)

Adela's scientific rationalism, epitomized by the field-glasses which will be broken in the caves, and her desire to see the 'real' India, is subtly undercut in a passage which subtextually recalls commentaries on the Hindu *Vedanta* suggesting an iconography in which the world is a serpent and the Brahman is a rope: the world, that is to say, is neither real nor unreal.

Through this kind of continuously creative instability of effect the novel seeks to reflect the unsettling of Western assumptions. In his 1918 declaration of the Fourteen Points, the American President Wilson had spoken of the need for 'A free, open-minded and absolutely impartial adjustment of all colonial claims'. Such a programme, in conjunction with Lenin's attack on imperialism, the formation at the end of the Great War of the Sinn Fein movement in Ireland, and the foundation of the League of Nations, exerted a powerful if gradual effect upon the groundswell of Indian nationhood. The Raj could never again tread upon such firm ground after the Great War, and Forster was perhaps uniquely well placed to perceive and register these tremors in his fiction. It is certainly clear that *A Passage to India* draws upon a mythology which may be designated Kiplingesque, most notably in its presentation of the scenes at the Club. Leonard Woolf, who had worked as a colonial officer in Ceylon, described these clubs as the 'symbol and centre of British imperialism'. The Club, he recalled, 'had normally an air of slight depression, but at the same time exclusiveness, superiority, isolation'. The atmosphere, he recalled, 'was terribly masculine and public school'. Within such institutions, Forster observed in wartime Egypt, the administrators flourished in an atmosphere of 'racial arrogance', an arrogance both reflected and created by the potently mythic colonial world presented to the reading public at home. In Kipling centrally, Forster argued, 'is a writer of great genius whose equipment has never developed', a writer who, most damagingly, 'inspects civilization as it were from the window of the Fifth Form room'. Nevertheless, the novel balances its attack upon the 'undeveloped heart', notably in its open acknowledgement of the difficulties inherent in Ronny Heaslop's position:

Every day he worked hard in the court trying to decide which of two untrue accounts was the less untrue, trying to dispense justice fearlessly, to protect the weak against the less weak, the incoherent against the plausible, surrounded by lies and flattery. (p. 69)

It may be worth recalling here the testimony of another writer who worked as a colonial administrator, George Orwell, writing about the service in 1942:

> It may be that all that they did was evil, but they changed the face of the earth ... whereas they could have achieved nothing, could not have maintained themselves in power for a single week, if the normal Anglo-Indian outlook had been that of, say, E. M. Forster.

The question of balance, in a work of social and political significance, may be crucial. For the distinguished American critic, Lionel Trilling, *A Passage to India* triumphantly achieved that balance; it is a judgement which deserves the deepest consideration:

> What distinguishes it from the patterns of similarly public and political novels is the rigour of its objectivity; it deals with unjust, hysterical emotion and it leads us, not to intense emotions about justice, but to cool poise and judgement – if we do not relent in our contempt for Ronny we are at least forced to be aware that he is capable of noble, if stupid, feelings; the English girl who has the hallucination of an attempted rape by a native has engaged our sympathy by her rather dull decency; we are permitted no easy response to the benign Mrs Moore, or to Fielding, who stands out against his own people, or to the native physician who is wrongly accused. This restraint of our emotions is an important element in the book's greatness.

This raises issues which each reader must finally decide for him or herself. Towards the end of the novel, the narrator remarks that the characteristic weakness of the East is suspicion, and that of the West, hypocrisy. The novel demonstrates how mankind aspires to comprehend the universe, an aspiration which has led to widely differing codes of belief and unbelief. Forster is careful not to trade on the stereotypes of the mysterious East and the materialist West: Mrs Moore is as profoundly mystical as Professor Godbole, Aziz as eager for success as Heaslop. However, the novel does suggest the equivocal strangeness of India and the passivity which may result from the vastness of an alien nature, a passivity perhaps finally endorsed in the acceptance of the Hindu ritual. There is a sense of strain in those characters who wish rationally to understand India, as in the analysis of Adela's thought-processes on the train to the Marabar. Such a passage traces the boundaries of the well-ordered Western mind, in its depiction of the intrusiveness of the bustling train which dwindles to insignificance within a landscape which swallows up its activity. This contrast is reproduced in human terms during the trial, as Adela observes the labours of the punkah-wallah:

he scarcely knew that he existed and did not understand why the court was fuller than usual, indeed he did not know that it was fuller than usual, didn't even know he worked a fan, though he thought he pulled a rope. Something in his aloofness impressed the girl from middle-class England, and rebuked the narrowness of her sufferings. In virtue of what had she collected this roomful of people together? Her particular brand of opinions, and the suburban Jehovah who sanctified them – by what right did they claim so much importance in the world, and assume the title of civilization? (p. 221)

Caste-ridden, poverty-stricken India, at the margins of the narrative, is acknowledged, and the action tends to support the narrator's contention that the English will, in the end, like other invaders, be 'worked into its pattern and covered with its dust' (p. 215). The interconnectedness upon which Godbole insists in his seminal conversation with Fielding is gradually perceived by other characters. Aziz for example, when he moves to Mau, discovers Muslim shrines turned into Hindu temples and ceases to mind; Mrs Moore 'becomes' 'Esmiss Esmoor'. In both cases, in the deepening sensitivity to mystery on the part of Adela and Fielding, interconnection is endorsed as transcending racial boundaries. Trilling suggests that religion, in Forster, 'expresses, though it does not solve, the human mystery'. This is just, and it indicates very accurately the severe limitations of Anglo-India, whose symbols are the bungalows of the civil station and the field-glasses broken at the Marabar. Within a tropical land the narrative shows how the British invaders circulate 'like an ice-stream' (p. 88). They lack intellectual or emotional curiosity and openness of spirit, existing in accordance with a national myth which supports a mean-spirited obsession with power. The novel makes their position and limitations crystal clear, but moves beyond them in the dramatization of the relations between Fielding and Aziz. Fielding, the great liberal romantic, reverts at the end at least partially to the values of the Raj. The letter from Heaslop says, ' "I'm relieved you feel able to come into line with the Oppressors of India to some extent" ' (p. 302), and Fielding now sees his heroism over Aziz as a 'memento, a trophy' (p. 313). Aziz, equally, moves away into a more positively nationalistic position towards the end. The central strain felt in the novel between Aziz and Fielding is the strain imposed by imperialism, a corrupting influence which can never be totally ignored or expunged. For all the mystical union hinted at by Mrs Moore and Professor Godbole, the novel ends with a realistic statement of separation and difference. The central relationship peters out with a failure of energy which seems to reflect a passivity in the narrative voice itself. The number of separations or failed relationships – the separation of Ronny and Adela, the gaps in sympathy between Adela and Fielding, and Fielding's failure to satisfy Stella – and the virtual disappearance of Mrs Moore and Professor Godbole, suggest the impossibility of connection in this environment. That impossibility is most fully explored through Fielding and Aziz.

Fielding, an experienced liberal humanist who travels light, is the only permanent resident of Chandrapore who seriously develops Indian connections. From the moment of accepting the collar-stud from Aziz there is a bond between the two men, but the false notes often signalled in their conversation rise to the surface more markedly after the trial. Wishing to be with Aziz, Fielding perceives his duty to stay with Adela, and this prompts the Indian allegation that 'The English always stick together' (p. 235). Fielding's underlying failure, one which he acknowledges in himself, is essentially a failure to penetrate more deeply into the realities of India. In this sense the Marabar echo represents the central test of the ability of the English characters to sink beneath the surface and meet a more threatening and disturbing reality beneath. In a rejected portion of the manuscript, Fielding is described entering a cave and reciting lines from Milton's *Paradise Lost* and Meredith's 'The Woods of Westermain'. The response is always 'boum':

'Go to hell!' he shouted and scuttled out like an excitable schoolboy before the avalanche fell. He could hear it smashing on to the empty floor, and thought 'Anyhow it missed me that time!' How intimate in comparison was the sky. 'Bad places,' he thought, looking round him at the distended throats. Into that which resembled a cobra's, he chucked a stone, and the same sound gushed out and seemed to mortify the air.

The suggestion here and elsewhere in the caves sequence is that even nature appears to threaten Anglo-India because of the fear which the rulers project outwards. Reality and symbol interpenetrate here, as Meredith had indicated in 'The Woods of Westermain':

> but bring you a note
> Wrangling, howso'er remote
> Discords out of discords spin
> Round and round derisive
> din.

The echo attacks only those sensitive to Indian complexities.

Adela's belief in the sanctity of personal relations, Mrs Moore's in
an ultra-personal deity, and Fielding's bluff common sense; these
admirable qualities are put into question by the sub-continent.

In 1922, while working on *A Passage to India*, Forster observed
of the Indian situation, 'never in history did ill-breeding contribute
so much towards the dissolution of an Empire'. This feeling under-
pins the crucial scene after the failure of the Bridge Party when
Ronny Heaslop lectures his mother on the role of the colonial
officer. '"I am out here to work," [he tells her], "to hold this
wretched country by force. I'm not a missionary or a Labour
Member or a vague sentimental sympathetic literary man"' (p. 69).
There follows a significant paragraph of authorial reflection:

> He spoke sincerely, but she could have wished with less gusto. How
> Ronny revelled in the drawbacks of his situation! How he did rub it in that
> he was not in India to behave pleasantly, and derived positive satisfaction
> therefrom! He reminded her of his public-school days. The traces of young-
> man humanitarianism had sloughed off, and he talked like an intelligent
> and embittered boy. His words without his voice might have impressed her,
> but when she heard the self-satisfied lilt of them, when she saw the mouth
> moving so complacently and competently beneath the little red nose, she
> felt, quite illogically, that this was not the last word on India. One touch of
> regret – not the canny substitute but the true regret from the heart – would
> have made him a different man, and the British Empire a different institution.
> (p. 70)

Ronny is one of those, described by Forster elsewhere, who 'go
forth into a world that is not entirely composed of public-school
men or even of Anglo-Saxons'. This class of men go out 'with well-
developed bodies, fairly developed minds, and undeveloped
hearts' (*Abinger Harvest*, p. 15). At this point in the novel, these
reflections demand closer interrogation. Can it be true that 'one
touch of regret' would have changed the nature of British imperialism? It has been suggested that Forster hated imperial domineering
but had no specific quarrel with imperial domination. The stress
upon relationship and connection, which reaches its unifying climax
as the boats are upset during the Krishna festivities at Mau, endorses
the implicit project of the text. On its own terms, as part of the
creative 'faking' which Forster desiderates, in *Aspects of the Novel*,
as a necessary part of fiction, the novel fully embodies a pattern of
cultural collision and interconnection. From a different point of
view, however, it is possible to demand what exactly the relationships between Fielding, Aziz, Mrs Moore and Adela have done for

the marginally glimpsed, caste-ridden world of the punkah-wallah. The positives of the book, from this perspective, look cloudy and metaphysical as they are embodied in Professor Godbole and Mrs Moore. Through such characters, indeed, Forster attempts to transcend his own innately sceptical spirit. The reader of *A Passage to India* needs to come to terms with some of the issues raised by colonialism, however, and not allow the novel to process a readily assumed and easily consumed moral position. The critic D. S. Savage has remarked of the work:

The ugly realities underlying the presence of the British in India are not even glanced at and the issues raised are handled as though they could be solved on the surface level of personal intercourse and individual behaviour.

Yet the early critiques of the book written by Indian readers would tend to dispute this. An anonymous Indian reviewer of 1928, for instance, declared 'for the first time I saw myself reflected in the mind of an English author', and Bhupal Singh, writing ten years after publication, found the book 'refreshing in its candour, sincerity, fairness, and art'. It was a work, he held, which 'arrives at no solution and offers no explanation'. Like Chekhov, then, Forster could be admired for 'putting the question'. This laudatory view from within India was well expressed in the year of publication, in a review by the journalist St Nihal Singh:

it gives the impression that there is no such thing as an Indian, for the Muslim disdains the Hindu and is in turn hated by the Hindu and Hindus and Muslims alike are slack, prevaricating, not quite honest, unreliable, sexually loose – in a word, inefficient from every point of view. The author is, however, not content with such an exposé but mercilessly tears away the gaudy vestments and gew-gaws which Anglo-Indians, or 'Europeans' as they prefer to call themselves, have draped about themselves and displays a sight which will revolt some persons, shame others and enrage still others.

With the coming of Independence, Indian perceptions of the place and function of the novel hardened in interesting and suggestive ways, and this alteration of stance is epitomized in an *Encounter* article published in 1954 by the Indian writer, Nirad Chaudhuri, under the title 'Passage to and from India'. Chaudhuri begins by describing *A Passage to India* as 'possibly an even greater influence in British imperial politics than in English literature'. Although he finds the book 'quite openly a satire on the British official in India' and on the native population, he is especially critical of the book's failure to incorporate any treatment of nationalism. Forster is thus, he argues, led 'to waste his politico-ethical emotion on persons who don't deserve it'. Both groups of characters are, in his view, 'insignificant and despicable', and this is demonstrated by the 'incredible' scenes at the Club. 'As a class,' Chaudhuri recalls, 'British officials kept their heads.' The lack in Anglo-India was 'not in courage, but in intelligence'. The portrayal of Muslim and Hindu communities is equally open to question. Godbole appears to Chaudhuri not so much a serious exponent of Hindu philosophy as a 'clown', and he argues that Forster's chief blunder was in 'taking Muslims as the principal characters in a novel dealing with Anglo-Indian relations'. The circle surrounding Aziz in the novel 'belong to the servile section of the Indian community' and are all 'inverted toadies'. Chaudhuri sums up his case against the novel thus:

It shows a great imperial system at its worst, not as diabolically evil but as drab and asinine; the rulers and the ruled alike are depicted at their smallest, the snobbery and pettiness of the one matching the imbecility and rancour of the other.

This is sweeping and perhaps unperceptive; certainly the reader should place against such judgement the consistent honesty of the text in its striving for connection. When Aziz encounters Mrs Moore in the mosque he declares:

'You understand me, you know what I feel. Oh, if others resembled you!'
Rather surprised, she replied: 'I don't think I understand people very well. I only know whether I like or dislike them.'
'Then you are an Oriental.'   (p. 45)

Immediately after this exchange Aziz has to explain to the old lady that Indians are not allowed into the Club. Here as elsewhere the text is fully alive to the contradictions inherent in the colonial situation; such contradiction stems from the covert exploitation of power and violence. The novel is aware of this, but seeks to mitigate its effects through the assertion of the supreme value of relation. Thus it is that the novel cleverly circles back, in the interview between Aziz and Ralph Moore, to the encounter at its beginning. Aziz has treated Ralph harshly:

'Don't you think me unkind any more?'
'No.'
'How can you tell, you strange fellow?'
'Not difficult, the one thing I always know.'
'Can you always tell whether a stranger is your friend?'

'Yes.'

'Then you are an Oriental.' (p. 306)

The implication here, as in the scenes between Aziz and Fielding, is that the divisions between races, as between classes or individuals, can be resolved through 'the secret understanding of the heart' expressed in Aziz's Persian poem. The novel draws here upon the ideology of liberalism, with its belief in the transcendent virtue of the individual. More specifically, Forster is indebted here as elsewhere in his work to the Edwardian social prophet, Edward Carpenter. Carpenter saw relationship as the panacea for the social ills of contemporary England:

The only road back to sanity is through the re-mingling of classes and masses, and the large readoption of the modes of life, thought and speech still current among the latter.

Sexual love, Carpenter argued, is 'a sentiment which easily passes the bounds of class and caste'. In his unconscious zest for life Aziz resembles earlier Forsterian characters such as Gino, young George Emerson, Stephen Wonham and Alec Scudder. Unlike *Maurice*, however, *A Passage to India* exposes this belief in the value of personal relations both to the nihilism of the caves and to the all-encompassing mystic Hinduism of Professor Godbole and Mrs Moore. The suggestion implicit in the final evocation of Gokul Ashtami is of a beneficent over-arching reality whose beneficence encompasses and negates the sterility of the Marabar echo, as Whitman had suggested in 'Passage to India':

Nature and Man shall be disjoin'd and diffused no more,
The true son of God shall absolutely fuse them.

Forster proceeds by cunning indirection, and it is typical of his method that the transcendent moment of vision ends as the rain 'settled in steadily to its job of wetting everybody and everything through' (p. 310). As Aziz and Fielding take their final ride together, each of them 'hardened since Chandrapore' (p. 314), their unity is riven by the fact that Fielding is one of the 'Army of Occupation'. Aziz excitedly cries, '"Down with the English anyhow"' (p. 315). When '"every blasted Englishman"' is driven into the sea, he declares, '"then you and I shall be friends"'. As yet, the text insists, the time is not ripe: 'the temples, the tank, the jail, the palace' in a hundred voices say no, '"No, not yet,"' and the sky says '"No, not there"' (p. 316).

This poetic and indeterminate postponement, though rhetorically persuasive, masks the indeterminacy of political viewpoint. In insisting upon a social and historical context for the novel, a context which supersedes the claims of Forsterian criticism, and desiring to resist Forster's description of the book as 'philosophical and poetic', it is necessary to evoke here Fredric Jameson's concept of the political unconscious of the text. The distinction between cultural texts which are political and others which are not, Jameson argues, is untenable. It is a spurious distinction which issues out of the pervasive 'privatization of contemporary life' of which Forster's own work may be a significant record. Such a distinction, Jameson argues in *The Political Unconscious*,

reconfirms that structural, experiential and conceptual gap between the public and the private, between the social and the psychological, or the political and the poetic, between history or society and the 'individual'.

An idealist or humanist approach which endorses the supremacy of the cultural product stealthily ignores the fact that there is nothing 'sheltered from the omnipresence of history and the implacable influence of the social'. Recognition of the political unconscious of the text will lead to the 'unmasking of cultural artifacts as socially symbolic acts'. With reference to *A Passage to India*, as to other texts, it is salutary to remind ourselves of Jameson's profound vision of history as 'ground and untranscendable horizon' within which all cultural products take their place.

The juxtaposition of *A Passage to India* with Frantz Fanon's powerful critique of colonialism, *The Wretched of the Earth*,* illuminates the strength and accuracy of Forster's portrait, but also exposes the significant silences in the text. The colonial world, Fanon argues, is 'a world divided into compartments'. The town of the settlers is 'strongly-built' and 'brightly lit', and 'the streets are covered with asphalt'. The Civil Station of Chandrapore, it will be recalled, 'is sensibly planned' with bungalows 'disposed along roads that intersect at right angles' (p. 32). The town of the colonized, says Fanon, is 'a crouching village, a town on its knees, a town wallowing in the mire'. Of Chandrapore, the narrator remarks, 'Houses do fall, people are drowned and left rotting, but the general outline of the town persists, swelling here, shrinking there, like some low but indestructible form of life' (p. 31). The colonized society is one 'cut in two' and 'inhabited by two different species', as Fanon describes it:

* Penguin Books, 1962.

It is neither the act of owning factories, nor estates, nor a bank balance which distinguishes the governing classes. The governing race is first and foremost those who come from elsewhere, those who are unlike the inhabitants, 'the others'.

This sense of otherness is both confirmed and challenged in the opening conversation between the Muslim group as to 'whether or no it is possible to be friends with an Englishman' (p. 33), and throughout the subsequent action. In Fanon's overview the principle of the colonial world is Manichean; it is a universe divided into energies of good and evil. The settler not only employs his power to delimit the status of the native, he possesses a vision of the native 'as a sort of quintessence of evil', 'insensible to ethics', one who represents the 'negation of values'. 'All values are in fact irretrievably poisoned and diseased as soon as they are allowed in contact with the civilized race.' During twenty-five years of colonial service, the Collector tells Fielding after the arrest of Aziz, ' "I have never known anything but disaster result when English people and Indians attempt to be intimate socially" ' (pp. 173–4). Similarly, McBryde expounds the theory that ' "All unfortunate natives are criminals at heart, for the simple reason that they live south of latitude 30" ' (p. 176). Of the period of nationalist consciousness prior to decolonization – exactly the historical situation of the novel – Fanon observes a dialogue beginning between colonized intellectuals and the colonial bourgeoisie, a dialogue concerned with 'values': 'The colonialist bourgeoisie, when it realizes that it is impossible for it to maintain its domination over the colonial countries, decides to carry out a rear-guard action with regard to culture, values, techniques and so on.' This is the role which, though presented unconsciously in the text, Fielding and Adela play in *A Passage to India*. Fielding is regarded as 'a disruptive force' by Anglo-India, believing as he does that the world is 'a globe of men who are trying to reach one another and can best do so by the help of goodwill plus culture and intelligence' (p. 80). It is perhaps significant that, for the first time in Forster's work, the limited efficacy of these Bloomsbury ideals is admitted, and they are profoundly exposed by the events at the Marabar. The evil in the caves, the loss of meaning and value which the echo effects in the sympathetic Europeans, is on one level consonant with the masked oppression and violence of colonialism. The native represents to the colonizer, Fanon suggests, 'the negation of values'; this negation is embodied in the caves, with their insistence upon nothingness.

The charge of attempted rape against the Indian doctor exactly parallels the Manichean tendency postulated by Fanon as a means of metamorphosing the native inhabitant 'into an animal'. One message of the caves might be of the crushing historical guilt of colonialism, which seeks to salve itself by imputing guilt, in the significant form of sexual conquest, to the colonized. Professor Godbole, indeed, expounds this theory of guilt to the uncomprehending liberal conscience of Fielding. When an ' "evil action is performed" ', he declares, ' "all perform it" ': ' "When evil occurs, it expresses the whole of the universe" ' (pp. 185–6). This scene is widely read as a mystical statement of Hindu unity of being. But taken together with the events at the Marabar, the contradictory nature and evil consequences of colonialism, and the complicity of the liberal-humanist project, stand unmasked through the metaphorical unconscious of the text. Fanon argues:

The well-known principle that all men are equal will be illustrated in the colonies from the moment that the native claims that he is the equal of the settler. One step more, and he is ready to fight to be more than the settler. In fact, he has already decided to eject him and to take his place; as we see it, it is a whole material and moral universe which is breaking up.

It is precisely this breaking up which *A Passage to India* explores in the full contradictions of its textual poetry.

The critical reception of the novel and varieties of interpretation

When *A Passage to India* was published in June 1924, it was received with enthusiasm by reviewers. Forster had returned to fiction, after fourteen years, with a novel that was regarded as his best to date, and there was widespread praise for the quality of his writing and characterization.

The critical reception of works of literature, and subsequent varieties of interpretation, bear witness to the manifold possibilities that many works offer, and indeed, the openness to a range of interpretation is often adopted as one criterion for judging whether something is 'literature' or not. In another sense, literature is always partly constructed by the reader, who brings meaning to a piece of writing. We read into it certain ideas and conclusions that are dictated not only by our own personal interests but also by our social position in terms of race, class and gender, and by the historical moment through which we are living. It is therefore inevitable that any given novel will be read differently at different times after its publication, and by different people. *A Passage to India* has been subject to a wide variety of interpretation, which demonstrates how it is a resonant and suggestive piece of fiction; the changing focus of readers' attention also indicates how the novel's context has changed over the years since 1924.

When *A Passage to India* was first published, the reviews generally ignored two areas of the novel: the caves, and the significance of the third section of the novel. The caves were usually regarded by reviewers as the catalyst that created the rumpus of the trial and its aftermath, rather than explored as the expression of some kind of nihilism or despair. Only two reviews attempted to consider them in more detail. John Middleton Murry intelligently surmised that the 'message' of the caves cast severe doubt on whether Forster would ever feel able to write another novel: 'A cave of Marabar is the symbol of the universe for Mr Forster: no wonder then that he should have waited so long before inviting an echo from it. He might almost as well have waited an eternity.' And Rebecca West chose to concentrate on the symbolism of the caves in the context of the novel as a whole:

a poem about the caves ... in the end creates a symbol of that willingness to imagine an eternity that is not motherly, an infinity which is not kind, an absolute that is not comforting, which makes certain forms of Indian mysticism terrifying to the Western mind.

Although the artistry of the novel was frequently praised, the features of the structure, and echoing in the novel, did not receive very much attention. Leonard Woolf was almost alone in stressing the 'layered' effect: beyond the story of Adela and Mrs Moore wishing to see the 'real' India, he said, there is

an arch of politics, the politics of Anglo-India and the nationalist India. And beyond that is another arch, half mystery, half muddle, which permeates India and personal relations and life itself... So the book builds itself up, arch beyond arch, into something of great strength, beauty, and also of sadness. The themes are woven and interwoven into a most intricate pattern, against which, or in which, the men and women are shown to us pathetically, rather ridiculously, entangled.

L. P. Hartley was moving in the same direction when he noted that '*A Passage to India* is much more than a study of racial contrasts and disabilities. It is intensely personal and ... intensely cosmic.' But apart from these comments, the main focus for reviewers was the relationship between British and Indians in India, and it was generally agreed that the novel was pessimistic in tone. This focus helps to explain why the third section of the novel was disregarded, or met with some impatience on the part of the reviewers.

Coming so comparatively soon after the massacre of Indians at Amritsar, and immediately following a lawsuit in England which rehearsed details of that event, *A Passage to India* was perceived as catching the 'Psychological Moment', as one reviewer put it. It was called 'a political document of the first importance', and elsewhere, readers were told '[Politics] give this novel half at least of its value'. The novel tackled, for these readers, the difficult subject of 'race feeling', an 'almost fratricidal subject', and, on the whole, Forster was considered to have managed the topic with impressive objectivity and fairness. It is interesting that American reviews of the novel, addressed to a readership which might be expected to have less partisan interest in the issue of the British presence in India, repeatedly emphasized the lack of bias in Forster's treatment of his theme.

Matters became more complex when attention turned to the questions of 'truth' or 'reality' in the portrayal of the characters. The portrayal of Aziz was commended for being conducted in a sympathetic way that avoided shadowy caricature, and Aziz was also considered truly convincing as an individual and as a representative Indian. For example, one reviewer said:

The Indians in this book are not, as in all other Anglo-Indian novels, deplorable but unavoidable pieces of the scenery. They are not cast for the roles of simple villains or clowns. They are men with different conventions from Englishmen – how different has never been revealed before.

The *Birmingham Post* commented, 'Aziz impresses one as the most absolutely "real" Indian to be found in fiction: a living son of that baffling people'. This approbation of the presentation of Aziz was not confined to the English reviews. In the *Times of India*, readers were told:

We have never encountered a more finished study of the psychology of Educated India – deft, incisive, sympathetic, but disillusioned. The mental complexes and inhibitions; the mysticism; the modernism; the racial pride; the intellectual alertness; the supersensitiveness, are all there. We are frankly amazed at the skill with which the scalpel is used to lay bare, as it were, each quivering nerve and to expose every morbid growth.

But these comments tend to muddle the convincingness of the

techniques of characterization with questions of verisimilitude, and of Aziz's Indianness and representativeness. It is possible, for example, that readers will agree that Aziz is convincingly drawn as an individual but will strongly disagree about whether he is either a convincing Indian or representative of Indians. The case is similar when we consider the portrayal of Anglo-Indians. Rose Macaulay was alert to the implications of how the novel might appear to readers of different races and experiences. In her review, she described Forster as a sympathetic and imaginative novelist, but concluded cryptically, 'But I should like very much to know what Anglo-Indians will think of it'.

Many Anglo-Indians did react very strongly to the novel. They did not object to the portrayal of the Indians, but complained that Forster's knowledge of India was limited at best, and inaccurate at worst. E. A. Horne, a member of the Indian Education Service, wrote in a letter to the *New Statesman* that the Anglo-Indians were 'wildly improbable and unreal', and said, 'it is a thousand pities that Mr Forster did not see the real Anglo-India, for he would have written an incomparably better and truer book; and we venture to suggest to him, next time he goes to India: "Try seeing Anglo-Indians"'. The court scene was generally criticized by this section of Forster's readership for its inaccuracies in procedure and mood. And a review in the Calcutta *Englishman* remarked that fiction about the relationship between British and Indians carries heavy responsibilities, because it cannot avoid 'some shade of political implication', and because fiction tends to be extremely influential in forming opinions. The review concluded, after listing some of Forster's inaccuracies in detail and mood:

Enough has been said to show how spurious an acquaintance with the facts of the inter District life the novelist presumes to draw on; and the exposure of the ludicrous may do something to counteract the injurious tendencies of this type of fiction.

Another Anglo-Indian dwelt on the pessimistic message of the novel for the future of British India. He went on to ask:

But if this is, as I am convinced it is, the moral for us of *A Passage to India*, I wonder what moral will be discernible by Mr Forster's Indian friends . . . Mr Forster's Indians are all miserable creatures, feeble, fawning, dishonest, treacherous, or what not. True, they are shown usually, though not entirely, in relation to Anglo-Indians. But the fact is there, and here is the point: we knew enough of Mr Forster's intellectual character and attitude to know that he must depict the representatives of the ruling race with severity; and we assumed that, of necessity, he would find examples of contrasted nobleness among the Indian people. He has not done so; and I suspect that to-day in the clubs of Anglo-India the *Sahih-log* are asking derisively what need there can be of a defence for their own position and behaviour, if this is all that their merciless critic has to say for the educated Indian.

What *did* Indians tend to feel about *A Passage to India*? It is, of course, impossible to generalize, but some examples of Indian reaction are illuminating. 'An Indian', writing in the *Nation and Athenaeum*, conceded that Forster's portrayal of Indians was by no means flattering, but praised Forster for breaking the stranglehold of superficial clichés about India and Indians propagated in previous Anglo-Indian fiction, for getting to know Indians as people, and for presenting Indians to a Western readership as 'ordinary human beings'. St Nihal Singh, on the other hand, objected to the possibility that in the portrayal of the Indians another inaccurate stereotype had been created. But he argued that the exposé of the Anglo-Indian community, in his opinion most accurate and revealing, would counteract this flaw, and that the novel raised political questions:

I wonder if the book will open the eyes of the British people. I see that it is being widely reviewed in the London and the provincial press, and the critics are writing of it in glowing terms. I have not seen it pointed out anywhere, however, that the author has come to realise that Anglo-Indians are acting in the manner in which he has described them as acting because they are determined to hang on to India and because they feel that that is the only way they can hang on. The problem, in other words, is not social, but political, and therefore, no end of homilies can have any effect upon improving the manners of the British in India. The political elevation of Indians is the only remedy which can cure them of their habit of looking down upon us – of belittling our past and our capacity – of desiring to keep us at a distance.

A Passage to India, coming at the time it did, and with its immediate subject, aroused strong feelings in some quarters: about the Indian question, about the power of fiction to influence public opinion, and about an author's social and political sympathies as expressed through his or her fiction. The novel did not, however, fail to be widely read and enjoyed, and it has been very popular with general readers ever since its publication. A less immediate and more measured response to Forster's work developed with the growth of academic criticism, especially in the 1950s and 1960s. Forster's status as a writer, and academic criticism itself, have grown in importance side by side. Attention has focused on other aspects of *A Passage to India*, and there are now many studies on various features of Forster's work. Some of those approaches will now be summarized, to display the richness of the novel, and the diversity of critical views that is possible.

Lionel Trilling's influential monograph on Forster, published in 1943, begins with the statement, 'a consideration of Forster's work is ... useful in time of war'. Indeed, the war caused many readers to reread and reassess works of literature in the light of immediate concerns, often in a search for consolation, instruction or imaginative escape. Another example of this tendency is George Orwell, who turned his attention to Charles Dickens in 1939, and produced a thoughtfully new account of Dickens's work. Trilling, an American critic, discussed Forster's work in the context of his liberal humanism, because, 'He is one of the thinking people who, in bad times, will not become less'. Trilling began a movement to read *A Passage to India* less as an Anglo-Indian novel than as a novel about the predicaments of humanity, infused with Forster's own liberal priorities: 'Forster's book is not about India alone; it is about all of human life.'

This trend has continued, and *A Passage to India* is often seen as a novel which transcends its immediate subject matter to engage, using that subject as metaphor, with a more general state of existence, and with philosophical questions. Thus, on this kind of reading, the novel is considered to deal with personal relations, with the human being's encounter with spiritual forces, with religious frames of mind, or with the conflicts between matter and spirit, separation and unity, reason and love. In addition, if the local plot of the novel is to be regarded as metaphorical, it is also possible to read Forster's portrayal of friendship between Englishman and Indian as being less immediately compelling than acting as an expression of the difficulties of friendship between men, a question which so preoccupied Forster personally.

A Passage to India is often discussed in the context of Forster's liberal humanism. The assumption here, on the part of critics, is that the novel has such an extensive dimension of philosophical issues that the author's own strongly held views are relevant to an understanding of the novel, and may be central to the discussion within the novel. If Fielding is the mouthpiece of the author, advocating 'goodwill plus culture and intelligence' (p. 80), then his successes and failures in making friends with Aziz and in living in India detached from partisan interests are an illustration of the extent to which liberal humanism can be effective. Many critics, in pursuing this line of inquiry, conclude that Forster admits more strongly than ever before the dimension of mysticism that rationalism and liberal humanism cannot confront. Fielding's awareness that he has missed something in life may be attributed to the muddle of India which defeats Western notions of proportion, or to his belief in 'travelling light' at the expense of emotion and love, or to his inability to understand the appeal of Eastern ways of thought, as evidenced in his incomprehension of Hinduism in the 'Temple' section. In this reading, then, *A Passage to India* becomes Forster's most serious questioning of liberal humanism, and an admission that it cannot be fully, or truly, effective.

The caves, and the 'worms' of sound within them, have received considerable commentary, usually as being presences in the novel which may nullify humanist priorities. They have been regarded, variously, as demonstrations of Hindu faith, as Jungian caves where the visitor is confronted with his or her own shadow, or self, or as the historical expression of pointlessness that, in 1924, gives the lie to liberal humanism prevailing after the Great War. On the other hand, their power to cause disillusionment has been turned back on the characters who encounter the echo in the caves: some readers feel that Forster is being ironic about nihilism and that Mrs Moore's and Adela's experiences demonstrate their own respective failures rather than a pervasive spirit of disillusion. The caves, in this interpretation, sometimes become a mirror of the visitor's temperament and mood, and not an all-conquering refusal to accord significance. Thus Mrs Moore is already irritable and impatient with personal relationships, and feels that her Christianity is inadequate to India, when she enters the caves. Adela is muddled about questions of physical attractiveness, marriage and love, and her position in the Anglo-Indian community, and she emerges with an accusation of assault which queries racial and sexual roles, and which effectively disqualifies her from becoming a memsahib. The novel, on this reading, becomes an interrogation of the limitations of human beings, personal relations and religious systems, in the face of natural or universal phenomena such as the caves.

As the characters most closely connected with an impersonal world, through experience, or religion, or both, the figures of Adela, but more especially Mrs Moore and Godbole, are often discussed. The significance of their experiences, their roles in the novel, and the amount of authorial identification with their points of view, are widely disagreed upon. Is Mrs Moore to be seen as wrong or right in her responses? Is Godbole to be seen as the final ideal? There are no decisive answers, but the degree to which they are emphasized in a reading tends to determine how the novel is ultimately interpreted.

The 'Temple' section has also received considerable attention. Frequently described as comparatively lacking in dramatic or comic effect, and as being written in a different style from the rest of the novel, its presence and significance are now often seen to have to be explained. This approach emphasizes the unity of the novel itself, and imposes upon the critic the task of discerning the wholeness and meaningful pattern of a work of art perceived as being organic. The confrontation between Anglo-Indians and Indians over the events at the Marabar Caves no longer appears to be the central issue of the novel, for that story virtually ends at the close of the 'Caves' section, with the exit of Adela and Mrs Moore. Instead, questions of Hinduism, spiritual unity, and the friendship between Aziz and Fielding are drawn out. There are possibilities of interpreting the novel as a defence of Hinduism, and sometimes Mrs Moore is defined as having been an instinctive Hindu throughout (although this approach lays less emphasis on precisely *how* we are to understand her experience in the caves). Other critics suggest that the novel ends on tentative notes of spiritual unity through the festival of Gokul Ashtami and the capsizing of the boats, although Aziz and Fielding cannot personally resume their closeness.

Forster's 'message' is not so much described as questioned by another group of critics, who bring a Marxist reading to the novel. Forster's habit of emphasizing the personal, and of drawing conclusions about the public and the social through characters and personal relations, is countered by them with the observation that this kind of equation is unsound, for it relies on an assumption that what happens in the personal realm has an effect on wider social and political issues. This reading is not merely a prejudiced account. It draws out the paradox that the realist novel habitually makes claims for the significance of the individual, and so we read *A Passage to India*, accordingly, as a work in which Forster suggests that Fielding's priorities and Mrs Moore's religion, for example, are meaningful beyond what they bring to that particular character. But Forster seems to defeat his own novelistic strategies by concluding that the individual is *not*, ultimately, of significance. (This approach relies on an interpretation of the novel as essentially pessimistic, the 'message' of the caves being seen as central to the meaning.)

Most readers attempt, at least, to decide to their own satisfaction whether the novel is pessimistic or optimistic. The final paragraph appears to afford proof to adherents of both points of view. From a position which sees the conclusion as negative, it can be argued that the impossibility of friendship is not only because of the British presence in India, but is also confirmed by the earth and the sky. On the other hand, the words, ' " No, not yet, ... No, not there" ', suggest that friendship *is* possible in another time and place. The division among readers on this point is also enacted in the decision about which aspect of the writing of the novel to focus upon: for example, those who are interested in the art and form of *A Passage to India* will tend to regard the very art and form as evidence of Forster's desire to believe in wholeness and unity. Those who are more interested in the statements within the novel are more likely to conclude that even the most sustained effort at unity is defeated (the telling reference here being to Godbole's inability to include the stone in his religious ecstasy). Some readers suggest that there are at least two major levels to the novel: the realm of personal relations, where people try to live with each other with varying degrees of success, and the realm of the impersonal, figured as India, nature, or the sky. The two levels interact, of course, but it is possible to argue that Forster shows failure and separation in the human world, but unity and meaning in the wider universe. Such a twofold interpretation often brings in the disjunction between realism and symbolism, inferring that the realistic dimension is equated with pessimism, and the symbolic with optimism. But Forster's irony allows the reader to rest on the conclusion that Forster never satisfactorily resolves the tensions in the novel, and indeed, does not wish to.

An emphasis on the structure and symbolism of *A Passage to India*, which has been one of the more popular approaches in recent years, relies on the conviction that Forster's techniques in themselves embody his themes. The common expression of this is that form and subject cannot be divided from each other. Consequently, an analysis of the technical features of the novel will lead to insights in interpretation. The movement of the novel from 'Mosque' to 'Caves' to 'Temple' can therefore be read as illustrative of the 'message', and it has been interpreted as, for example, a movement from attempts to connect, through the destruction of all such attempts, to a transcendent harmony. Alternatively, some readers see less of a development than a tripartite statement of different ways of seeing the world: there are some difficulties here, but examples of this approach are that the three sections may portray Islam ('Mosque'), Christianity ('Caves') and Hinduism ('Temple'), or that they portray Anglo-India ('Mosque'), India before imperialist conflict ('Caves') and the India to come ('Temple'). Such patterning of the novel is also read into the recurrence of certain symbols, ranging from the wasp and the caves to the echoes in the caves and what they signify, which themselves create the echoing of phrases, shapes and symbols, such as arches and grids, within the form of the novel.

Some readers conclude that the novel has many layers. Andrew Rutherford describes it as 'at once a historical document, a philosophical statement, and a work of conscious literary art'. This has the effect of releasing us into choosing which aspect to enjoy most in the novel, and allows for the diversity of interpretation which is so noticeable when talking of *A Passage to India*. However, some readers begin their inquiry at this point, asking whether the novel is basically traditional, or basically modernist, in themes and techniques. In this approach, the contexts within which we are to read *A Passage to India* come to the fore again. Are we to regard the novel as a late example of the novel of society, depicting characters in relation to each other, or are we to regard it as experimental in form and technique and twentieth century in its vision of despair? This way of regarding the novel moves outwards to place the novel within historical and literary contexts, but also has a determining effect on what aspects of the novel we will find particularly significant.

8. Appendix: Forster's other novels

Forster had written five novels and a number of short stories before he came to write *A Passage to India*. They are all different and deserve to be read for themselves, and therefore should not be considered as preparatory exercises before the achievement of *A Passage to India*; however, in their themes and in the forms of the novels, we see some of the elements that are developed or changed in the last novel. The following discussion of Forster's other novels will, therefore, focus on those aspects which are particularly relevant to a reading of *A Passage to India*.

Forster's first novel, published in 1905 when he was twenty-six, was *Where Angels Fear to Tread*. It was generally well received, the reviewers commenting on the 'originality of conception and attitude', and noting its themes as being 'a protest against the worship of conventionalities', a 'study of national temperaments in conflict', and 'those challenges of ultimate things which are rarely faced in the even flow of an orderly world'. It tells of how a young English widow escapes from her late husband's stifling family by impulsively marrying an Italian ten years younger than herself, and settling down with him in a small town in Tuscany. The marriage is not happy, and Lilia dies in giving birth to a son. Her first husband's family, having tried to prevent the marriage, now attempt to claim the baby, blundering into the Italian way of life 'where angels fear to tread'. Two of the English characters, Philip and Caroline, are humbled by their encounter with a different culture and race; the third, Harriet, steals the baby, who is almost immediately killed in an accident. Gino, the Italian husband and father, attacks Philip when told of his son's death, but there is eventually a reconciliation between the two men, before Philip returns to England.

Christopher Gillie has suggested that one of Forster's distinctive characteristics as a novelist is 'his use of criteria for living still available in certain foreign cultures but lost to, or dormant in our own, so establishing a critical standpoint for assessing English ways of life'. This could be extended into the observation that Forster is also interested in versions of Englishness and the way that the English regard, and react to, the idea of 'abroad'. In this first novel, he shows different ideas of 'abroad'. When Lilia is leaving Charing Cross, 'abroad' is an escape from the rigidity of Sawston life: Sawston, here and in *The Longest Journey*, is Forster's name both for a specific place – Tonbridge – where he was unhappy at school, and for a more general social environment which is narrow minded and intolerant. When Lilia reaches Monteriano, Italy and 'abroad' signify romance, and so she marries one of the inhabitants. To Harriet, who takes her holidays in Protestant Switzerland, Italy represents a threat to all things English and Protestant, while to Philip it is the attractive but safely distant culture which enables him to be a daring iconoclast in Sawston without ever actually rejecting the English way of life. It is also, most importantly, the liberating breath of life that transforms Caroline and that gives Philip, finally, at least a glimpse of the possibilities of living. Forster portrays Italian life primarily as an opposition to stifling Sawston values, and defines it largely in terms of its difference from English ways of life. He only partly develops a portrayal of Italian life as an autonomous and distinct way of living: for example, at one point he comments that the much-vaunted freedom of the Italian male in his approach to existence is only possible at the expense of the freedom of Italian women but the point is not developed. The encounter between the English and the Italians gives plenty of opportunity for comedy, although the comedy is always in the reactions of the English, who have a lot of learning to do, and not on the part of the Italians, whose lives are, on the whole, untouched by these interlopers. One example here is the visit to the opera at Monteriano made by Philip, Harriet and Caroline. During the overture, 'The audience accompanied with tappings and drummings, swaying in the melody like corn in the wind. Harriet, though she did not care for music, knew how to listen to it. She uttered an acid "Shish!"' (*Where Angels Fear to Tread*, p. 103). Harriet keeps the audience in order for a while, but is finally routed by the enthusiasm of the Italians. However, the Italians are not portrayed as being completely 'good' as opposed to the stiffness of the English. Their tendency to behave spontaneously is associated, by Forster, with disorder and even violence, so that Lilia, during her brief, unhappy marriage, comes to yearn for the settled domesticity and security of Sawston.

Forster provides different versions of 'Englishness' in his English characters: the intolerance and rigidity of Mrs Herriton and Harriet, who despise 'abroad', the stiffness and emotional coldness of Philip, who can sense other alternatives, and the potential for life in Caroline, which has been suffocated in Sawston under the social environment and her involvement in 'good works'.

Italy, in this novel, is represented as that which is 'different': a different terrain, a different religion, and of a different age. The Italian countryside is attractive but alien. The grove of violets on the way from the station represents a typically Forsterian enclosure of vitality, freedom and disorder, but when Lilia tries to escape from Gino, she is thwarted by the terrain. The Roman Catholic church provides the occasion of some satire at Harriet's expense; however, it is not examined as a coherent system of faith, but more importantly comes to represent a disorder which is somewhat similar to the Hindu festival at the end of *A Passage to India*. The Italians in this novel are still living in the Middle Ages. While Philip and Caroline are able to travel across continents subject only to the inconveniences of the railway system, the journey from the station to the town is one of difficulty as the modern world is left behind.

As in most of his novels, Forster creates a central situation – here, the marriage of Lilia and Gino and the birth of their child – only to divert attention away from this traditional fictional focus on heterosexual personal relations, in order to consider the effects on bystanders, usually English and male. Lilia and Gino cannot be happy together because 'No one realized that more than personalities were engaged; that the struggle was national; that generations of ancestors, good, bad, or indifferent, forbade the Latin man to be chivalrous to the northern woman, the northern woman to forgive the Latin man' (*Where Angels Fear to Tread*, p. 58). The barriers of sex and race combine to make the marriage impossible. Yet Gino and Philip almost thrive on the difference between the races:

the two young men parted with a good deal of genuine affection. For the barrier of language is sometimes a blessed barrier, which only lets pass what is good. Or – to put the thing less cynically – we may be better in new clean words, which have never been tainted by our pettiness or vice. Philip, at all events, lived more graciously in Italian, the very phrases of which entice one to be happy and kind. (*Where Angels Fear to Tread*, p. 135)

The friendship which develops between the two men becomes the focus of the novel, reaching its climax in a notorious scene of violence where Gino tortures Philip for the death of his son, but is reconciled to him by the influence of Caroline.

A Room with a View, published in 1908, is the other novel by
Forster which is concerned with Italy. It is generally considered to
be Forster's most light-hearted and comic novel, partly because in
conception, though not in publication, it is the earliest of Forster's
novels, and partly because it has a conventionally 'happy ending'
with the marriage of Lucy and George. But as early as 1906, Forster
expressed a lack of sympathy with happy endings in contemporary
fiction: an earlier draft of the novel ended with a separation rather
than a marriage.

The plot here concerns the visit to Florence of Lucy and her
chaperone, Charlotte. Despite Charlotte's efforts, Lucy is exposed
to the unconventionality of two Englishmen, the Emersons, and to
the disorder of Italian life. She and George Emerson witness a
murder in the Piazza della Signoria, and later share a brief kiss on
a hillside outside Florence, whereupon she is hastily transported to
the safer environment of Rome by Charlotte. Back in England, in
the second half of the novel, Lucy consents to marry Cecil, a cold-
hearted and 'sneering' Englishman, but an encounter with George,
and a series of typically Forsterian coincidences, encourage her to
break away and marry George in the face of family disapproval.

In this novel, the encounter is not so much between Italian and
English people, as between different types of English people, some of
whom have been prodded into imaginative life by Italian experience.
Correspondingly, the Italians as a race are not portrayed in very
much detail, although their violence and spontaneity are suggested
in the scenes of the murder and of the two lovers who flirt while
driving a thoroughly mismatched party of English tourists into the
hills above Florence. But these scenes act primarily as a contrast to
the emotional paralysis of most of the English and the growing
spontaneity of Lucy and George.

Forster satirizes what he sees as an English tendency to withdraw
into rigid class structures when under siege in a different culture.
The novel opens in a very 'English' pension in Florence where
even the 'Signora' speaks cockney. 'Englishness' here is almost
impermeable to foreign influences, and the self-imposed constraints
of class and social behaviour among the English come to the fore.
Mr Emerson's first social misdemeanour is to offer his and his son's
rooms to the two English ladies. This forthrightness is defined by
the other tourists as socially unacceptable: 'She knew that the
intruder was ill-bred, even before she glanced at him' (*A Room with
a View*, p. 24). The English, according to Forster, exclude the

eccentric by invoking class distinctions. In *A Passage to India*, Fielding's joking 'aside to the effect that the so-called white races are really pinko-gray' (p. 80) has the similar effect of causing him to be somewhat distrusted by the Anglo-Indian community.

The English react in various ways to the influence of a different culture, and their reactions imply degrees of moral worth. Miss Lavish affects to like the 'real' Italy, but only uses it to emphasize a spurious unconventionality, and to write bad books about. Charlotte Bartlett feels threatened by it:

[Lucy] bought a photograph of Botticelli's *Birth of Venus*. Venus, being a pity, spoiled the picture, otherwise so charming, and Miss Bartlett had persuaded her to do without it. (A pity in art of course signified the nude.) (*A Room with a View*, p. 61)

Lucy herself is confused and overwhelmed, disliking bad smells, but attracted to the romantic views and promise of freedom. Yet her 'bravery' in defying Charlotte and buying a reproduction of Botticelli's painting assumes its true proportion when the picture is splashed with the murdered man's blood: the 'real' escape is only for the courageous, for Italy involves murder, explosions and disillusionment. Mr Eager, the pompous chaplain to the English colony, is satirized when he says, ' "This very square – so I am told – witnessed yesterday the most sordid of tragedies. To one who loves the Florence of Dante and Savonarola there is something portentous in such desecration – portentous and humiliating" ' (*A Room with a View*, pp. 71–2). Mr Eager's idealization of Italian history conveniently overlooks the fact that Savonarola was hanged and burned for his heretical views in 'this very square' in 1498.

A Room with a View, depicting tourists' reactions to Florentine art, tends to measure the spiritual and moral worth of a character by his or her response to various well-known works of art. In a similar way, in *Howards End*, the reactions of characters to a performance of Beethoven's Fifth Symphony are keys to their respective sensibilities and views. In *A Passage to India*, the attitudes towards art and music traced by Forster are complicated by the lack of comprehension between East and West, and by relations of domination and oppression. However, Forster does still tend to convey a judgement about the taste of the British, for example, in their staging *Cousin Kate*; Ronny's embarrassment about having once played the viola and his impatience with Godbole's song at the end of Fielding's tea-party display the coercive narrow-mindedness of the British in India and Ronny's own lack of sensitivity. In addition, in both *Where Angels Fear to Tread* and *A Room with a View*, there are references to Baedeker, the tourist guide. It is regarded ambivalently by Forster as conveying to the imaginative the romance of Italy, but also as packaging culture into a safe and unthreatening form for tourists. The later desire of Adela and Mrs Moore to see the 'real' India is an honourable and imaginative desire, but neither can accept the intimations of a reality which is not available to mere tourists.

A Room with a View owes a great deal to the novels of Jane Austen, particularly in the way that the series of events is structured around social gatherings, beginning with the meal at the pension in the opening pages. There are two climaxes: the excursion into the hills above Florence, and the swimming party at the 'Sacred Pool'. Like, for example, the outing to Box Hill in *Emma*, or the walking party in *Persuasion*, the social gatherings are disastrous in terms of manners and individual behaviour, but they release the true spirit of life. It is in these mixed encounters, where social rules are violated, but where some human beings reach communication with one another, that Forster portrays the simultaneous distress, liberation, violence and illumination that form the basis of his view of the world. The outing into the hills creates the circumstances where George impulsively kisses Lucy. But: 'The silence of life had been broken by Miss Bartlett, who stood brown against the view' (*A Room with a View*, p. 89). This heterosexual encounter, which provides the marriage plot of the novel, is balanced by the scene of male camaraderie at the 'Sacred Pool', where Freddy, George and Mr Beebe strip, bathe together, and are liberated from constraints so that they play games in the woods, until they are interrupted by the arrival of Lucy, her mother and her fiancé. In *A Room with a View*, the forces of respectability almost succeed in quelling the upsurge of emotion and spontaneity.

A central concern of the novel is the semi-mystical expression of the importance of the emotions and of physical life, stated by Mr Emerson:

'love is of the body; not the body, but of the body. Ah! the misery that would be saved if we confessed that! Ah for a little directness to liberate the soul! Your soul, dear Lucy! I hate the word now, because of all the cant with which superstition has wrapped it round. But we have souls.' (*A Room with a View*, p. 223)

He places these values against the rules of propriety, the constraints of established religion, and the stale and dutiful responses of tourists to Italian art. This is a recurrent preoccupation in Forster's work. The intellect, in this novel, as in much of his writing, is in danger of becoming cold and lacking in sympathy. Its condescension is linked by Forster to class distinctions in English society, so that those of a lower class seem to have more access to emotion and physicality, while aridity and intellect go hand in hand unless the heart and body are developed equally with the mind.

Forster published *The Longest Journey* in 1907. The title is a quotation from Shelley's *Epipsychidion*, dwelling on the prospect of limiting one's friendships when one succumbs to the priority of an exclusive relationship: 'and so/With one chained friend, perhaps a jealous foe,/The dreariest and the longest journey go'. Rickie Elliott seeks love, companionship and friendship, but a misguided reverence for a moment of passion which he has witnessed between Agnes and her fiancé leads him to fall in love with, and marry, Agnes after the sudden death of her lover. The marriage brings not intimacy but constraint, and almost loses him his other friends and his illegitimate half-brother, Stephen. The novel explores the search for love, and the conflicting claims of exclusive marital relationships and 'friends, and work, and spiritual freedom' (*The Longest Journey*, p. 87), seeming to suggest that men desire wider circles of companionship than do women. Rickie has always longed for a brother; he eventually manages to shake off exclusivity and social propriety, and commits himself to a life with Stephen. The novel is a curious mixture of evolutionary determinism and mysticism, and owes much to the ideas of Edward Carpenter. Rickie, the product of mismatched parents, has inherited a disability, while Stephen, the product of a union of love, is healthy and instinctual: Rickie dies in the act of saving Stephen from being run over by a train. It seems that he therefore achieves love and companionship but loses the evolutionary battle.

In *The Longest Journey*, Forster presents three versions of Englishness. The novel opens with a scene at Cambridge, where Rickie is an undergraduate, and where the prevailing spirit is one of inquiry and tolerance. Friendships and disinterested debate flourish in this atmosphere. After his marriage, Rickie finds himself trapped in the suffocating atmosphere of Sawston, where he is drawn into the habits of intimidation and petty bureaucracy that Forster, throughout his writing, defines as the public-school spirit, personified here in the character of Herbert Pembroke. Herbert's definition of the acceptable kind of Englishman is precisely the kind of definition that Forster elsewhere uses as condemnation:

> 'If a man shoots straight and hits straight and speaks straight, if his heart is in the right place, if he has the instincts of a Christian and a gentleman – then I, at all events, ask no better husband for my sister.' (*The Longest Journey*, p. 52)

The third type of Englishness presented by Forster is the honest and instinctual life symbolized by Stephen, and by the open and sweeping plains of Wiltshire which are his natural habitat. Stephen rejects orthodox Christianity, and turns instinctively to Hellenic life; he rejects books in favour of the open air. As a child he had escaped, naked, on to the roof of Cadover:

> Mr Failing, who was sitting alone in the garden too ill to read, heard a shout, 'Am I an acro-terium?' He looked up and saw a naked child poised on the summit of Cadover. 'Yes,' he replied; 'but they are unfashionable. Go in,' and the vision had remained with him as something peculiarly gracious. He felt that nonsense and beauty have close connexions – closer connexions than Art will allow – and that both would remain when his own heaviness and his own ugliness had perished. (*The Longest Journey*, p. 125)

Rickie's journey is partly from an over-romanticized view of nature to an understanding of the uncompromising Wiltshire landscape and the life it fosters in Stephen. It is in Wiltshire that, eventually, he dies. Yet for much of the novel he is set apart – by his disability, his sensitivity, and his confusion.

Howards End, published in 1910, focuses on the English and on England's progress from being a traditional, essentially rural society to the fully developed industrialism of the twentieth century. It has been called Forster's 'Condition of England' novel. The encroachment of suburbia, the acceleration of life's rhythms, the growth of materialism, and the deracination of the individual all underlie the events of the novel. In *Howards End*, Forster portrays the ways in which Margaret and Helen Schlegel confront the Wilcox family, representatives of progress, automatization and materialism. After an initial attraction to this way of life, Helen becomes hostile, retreating to the position of valuing spontaneity, affection and truth above all else. Margaret, on the other hand, is more gradually attracted to the strength and confidence of the Wilcox ethos, marries Mr Wilcox, and endeavours to 'connect' her value of emotion with his unemotional, less enlightened, way of life. She recognizes that the life of the emotions can only be pursued if one is comfortably off, and therefore implicated in business life. This is borne out by the presence in the novel of the character Leonard Bast, who, because of his lack of money and his lower class, cannot afford gentility or spontaneity. Helen attempts to save Leonard from the 'abyss' of poverty, becomes pregnant by him, and tries to give him money; Leonard finally dies of heart failure, caused partly by Charles Wilcox. A tentative reconciliation between the Schlegels, the Wilcoxes, and Leonard's posthumous son closes the novel.

The publication of this novel heralded Forster's general acceptance as a writer of ability and note. In its attempt to convey a sense of widespread social and material change, it signifies some ambition on Forster's part to broaden his scope and to join a certain tradition of novel writing. His examination of the role of culture in social relations becomes more historically contextualized, and more tentative: while he is still concerned with the effects on the individual of either valuing or despising the life of the affections and the senses, he attempts in this novel to provide a sense of English tradition, and a span of English social life. The efforts of individuals to communicate with one another without restraint, across the barriers of class, sex, and value-system – Margaret and Mrs and Mr Wilcox, Helen and Paul, Helen and Leonard – are shown in the context of material differences which inevitably lead to relationships of power and oppression, both financially and sexually. 'Only connect', the epigraph of the novel, becomes not only an exhortation to make friends, but also the expression of a wish that the interrelatedness and mutual support within society be recognized, for the threads of responsibility and indebtedness stretch far beyond the individual's immediate circle. This was implicit in the earlier novels' plots of coincidence and violent outcome, but it is stated by Margaret in *Howards End*:

'Wilcoxes hadn't worked and died in England for thousands of years, you and I couldn't sit here without having our throats cut. There would be no trains, no ships to carry us literary people about in, no fields even. Just savagery. No – perhaps not even that. Without their spirit life might never have moved out of protoplasm. More and more do I refuse to draw my income and sneer at those who guarantee it.' (*Howards End*, p. 164)

As in *The Longest Journey*, Forster locates an English tradition in the landscape of Wiltshire, invoking a semi-mystical notion of nature. England is once again peopled by several different types, here deliberately distinguished also in terms of social class. The Wilcoxes are blunt, unimaginative and unemotional; the Schlegels, significantly half-German, value truth and love; Leonard Bast has been disinherited from the earth by progress, and is engaged in a struggle to survive, unable to appreciate culture because of his disadvantages. Forster's concern for the lower classes here is uneasy and enigmatic. In a notorious passage, he claims,

We are not concerned with the very poor. They are unthinkable, and only to be approached by the statistician or the poet. The story deals with gentlefolk, or with those who are obliged to pretend that they are gentlefolk.

The boy, Leonard Bast, stood at the extreme verge of gentility. He was not in the abyss, but he could see it . . . (*Howards End*, p. 44)

Forster is attempting to give his novel a dimension of social realism. However, such a portrayal of the lower classes sits uneasily with the symbolism, that Forster favours, of instinctual life and emotion in those of a lower class, which he uses in the characterization of the Emersons in *A Room with a View* and Stephen Wonham in *The Longest Journey*, and which he also discerns in those of a different race, such as Gino in *Where Angels Fear to Tread*.

Maurice was written by Forster in 1913 and 1914, after his first visit to India, out of an urgent need to write a homosexual novel which ended happily; it was not published until after his death in 1970. It deals very locally with the personal history of Maurice, who comes slowly and painfully to the realization that he is homosexual. He is awakened into consciousness at Cambridge by Clive Durham, an ascetic Hellenist with whom he develops a close but platonic relationship, until Clive becomes heterosexually oriented after an illness. The loneliness and alienation of Maurice are movingly depicted, as are his attempts to be 'cured' before he meets Alec Scudder, the gamekeeper on Clive's estate. Maurice and Alec eventually go to live together in the 'greenwood', the term for Maurice's (and Forster's) fanciful dream of a free England, liberated both emotionally and socially.

As in other of Forster's novels, music and art are used as touchstones, here as references to a series of homosexual traditions: Tchaikovsky, Plato and Michelangelo are all mentioned. Clive develops a theory about the emotional response of the homosexual to art:

'Look at that picture, for instance. I love it because, like the painter himself, I love the subject. I don't judge it with eyes of the normal man.

There seem two roads for arriving at Beauty – one is in common, and all the world has reached Michelangelo by it, but the other is private to me and a few more. We come to him by both roads.' (*Maurice*, p. 83)

The sense of otherness and the greater access to emotion, which Forster has identified in those of a different race and class, are here also identified in those of a different sexuality. Indeed, race, class and sex in Forster's work are all central and interrelated concerns in his exploration of communication and friendship.

Forster's interest in Englishness recurs in this novel, in the differing classes and emotional capabilities of the three main characters. Clive Durham, the landowner, embraces an ascetic and emotionally impoverished life, signifying the decay and decadence of the aristocracy, and the disregard for that life of the senses which Forster considers so important. Maurice is a complex character, who Forster stated is unlike himself, although some critics discern similarities. Maurice is a middle-class product of the public school system, well meaning but dull. His wakening is in the pattern of several Forsterian male characters, such as Philip Herriton and Rickie Elliott: it is a painful process of casting off conventional values and treasuring the heart's impulses. Maurice's suffering is described by Forster as 'the flesh educating the spirit ... developing the sluggish heart and the slack mind against their will' (*Maurice*, p. 139). Alec is another, rather unsuccessful, attempt on Forster's part to portray a member of the lower classes. He is sly, inarticulate, tender and unrefined. It is he who helps Maurice to come to terms with himself.

Nature in *Maurice* is depicted in two ways. To Maurice, and to Forster, it comes to stand for an ideal arena of fulfilment, where Maurice and Alec may be together forever. But it is also perceived as being disregarding and cruel in the face of human aspiration, and its evolutionary failures reflect the defeat of life in the human world. When Maurice, hoping to be cured, leaves Penge, he comes face to face with a row of blighted roses:

Blossom after blossom crept past them, draggled by the ungenial year: some had cankered, others would never unfold: here and there beauty triumphed, but desperately, flickering in a world of gloom. Maurice looked into one after another, and though he did not care for flowers the failure irritated him. Scarcely anything was perfect. On one spray every flower was lopsided, the next swarmed with caterpillars, or bulged with galls. The indifference of nature! And her incompetence! (*Maurice*, p. 165)

The idea that nature has somehow gone wrong is countered by the final appearance of Maurice in the novel, when he crushes the evening primroses, a symbol of his identification with the nocturnal side of English nature.

Perhaps the most moving aspect of *Maurice* for the reader interested in Forster's work as a whole is the depiction of Maurice's loneliness, and his longing for a friend. In a recurrent dream, Maurice imagines a friend:

He scarcely saw a face, scarcely heard a voice say, 'That is your friend,' and then it was over, having filled him with beauty and taught him tenderness. He could die for such a friend, he would allow such a friend to die for him; they would make any sacrifice for each other, and count the world nothing, neither death nor distance nor crossness could part them, because 'this is my friend.' (*Maurice*, p. 15)

In this context the friend signifies a homosexual partner and lover, yet it helps to explain the general emphasis in Forster's work on friendship. There is a complex exploration, in his work, of love, friendship, physical consummation and marriage, which is never resolved in any of the novels. Friendship is often problematic because of the barriers of language, race and class; scenes of male camaraderie are frequently disrupted by the intrusion of women; heterosexual relationships are fraught with the divisions of sex, and sometimes class. While some of the problems may be traced back to the inevitable pessimism of a homosexual writing in the early decades of the twentieth century, it is fairer to suggest that Forster is well aware of the barriers of sex, race and class to a true, satisfying and lasting communication between individuals, while at the same time, he constantly affirms the importance of communication.

In *A Passage to India*, Forster's interest, then, in Englishness, the English abroad, other races and cultures, the search for a friend, and nature, is continued and developed, and the novel adopts narrative techniques and strategies which are in many ways similar to those of the earlier novels. It is partly true to say that *A Passage to India* really *is* the culmination of Forster's consistent meditation on interaction and friendship between people of different races and classes, but the relationship between Indians and English is complicated by the relationships of subordination and domination created by imperialism. The Indians are not merely 'different' from the English, but are engaged in the tensions of imperialism; as one critic has described it, 'what it does to human beings in terms of distortion of perceptions: insensitivity, inhumanity on one side and degradation and cowardice on the other'. The Indian terrain, the Indian culture, are perceived as being totally alien, and here the Mediterranean becomes the measure of balance absent in the Eastern environment and psyche. On his arrival in India, Fielding had tried to 'regard an Indian as if he were an Italian' (p. 79), but when he stops at Venice on his way back to England, he realizes that

The buildings of Venice, like the mountains of Crete and the fields of Egypt, stood in the right place, whereas in poor India everything was placed wrong ... Writing picture-postcards to his Indian friends, he felt that all of them would miss the joys he experienced now, the joys of form, and that this constituted a serious barrier. (pp. 277–8)

In a similar way, the tendency of the English, which Forster has depicted in *A Room with a View*, to withdraw into rigid class structures and to reject foreignness, is exacerbated and reinforced by the physical and historical circumstances of the British in India. The opening chapter of the novel describes the division between the Indian Chandrapore and the Civil Station, which 'shares nothing with the city except the overarching sky' (p. 32): the division is geographical, architectural, social and philosophical. Justified as a necessity by the need to administer the empire, the distance maintained between the British and the Indians reveals the snobbishness and xenophobia of the British, and the disillusionment and dislike of the Indians. This is countered throughout the novel by the comments of Mrs Moore, ' "The English *are* out here to be pleasant" ' (p. 70), and of Aziz, ' "Kindness, more kindness, and even after that more kindness. I assure you it is the only hope" ' (p. 128), and by the attempts of Adela, Fielding, Mrs Moore and Aziz, variously, to communicate. In *A Passage to India*, Forster's message of communication assumes both personal and political implications. The novel is in a line of literature about the British in India which muses on precisely this question of how friendly the British should become with those they rule: an example is Kipling's collection of short stories, *Plain Tales from the Hills* (1888), where story after story depicts various types of relationships between the Indians and the British.

Within the Anglo-Indian community, the divisions of class are also apparent, created by the hierarchical social structure and by the tendency to exclude the eccentric; Adela and Fielding, for example, are both demoted in terms of class because they do not subscribe to the ethos wholeheartedly: 'Mrs Turton closed her eyes at this name and remarked that Mr Fielding wasn't pukka, and had better marry Miss Quested, for she wasn't pukka' (p. 49). It is Mrs Turton, too, who expresses in parodic form how the Anglo-Indians reject the Indians in terms of class: ' "You're superior to them, anyway. Don't forget that. You're superior to everyone in India except one or two of the ranis, and they're on an equality" ' (p. 61). Indeed, this aspect of the novel has led Lionel Trilling to identify the theme of separateness as the central theme of the novel: 'The separation of the English from the Indians is merely the most dramatic of the chasms in this novel'. The portrayal of the Anglo-Indian community, however, is a caricature of the English insularity depicted in the earlier novels. Forster is far less tolerant of the English as a community, and he demonstrates the serious implications for imperialism and justice as their snobbishness results in the hysterical reactions to Adela's experience, the violent arrest of Aziz, and the irrational behaviour of the Anglo-Indians in court.

As well as incorporating the political considerations of imperialism in this novel, Forster extends his emphasis on the emotional need for a friend, discussed in *The Longest Journey* and *Maurice*, until it becomes a transcendent image of human longing for communication with the spiritual. Godbole's song is the expression of a religious search pursued by many characters throughout the novel:

'I say to Shri Krishna: "Come! Come to me only." The God refuses to come. I grow humble and say: "Do not come to me only. Multiply yourself into a hundred Krishnas, and let one go to each of my hundred companions, but one, O Lord of the Universe, come to me." He refuses to come.' (p. 96)

It is in this context that nature, in *A Passage to India*, is a vast expanse, the 'overarching sky' an image both of nothingness and of ultimate unity: gone is the sense of physical locality and of familiar environment found in the earlier novels.

The spiritual and transcendent dimension of *A Passage to India*, which many critics focus upon, indicates that Forster's previous desire to write fiction along the lines of social realism has lessened. This is evident in his portrayal of class and society. Unlike the lower-class characters such as Stephen Wonham, Leonard Bast and Alec Scudder, who betray Forster's contradictory symbolic and realistic aims, the lower classes in this novel are not realistic characters, but are purely symbols of instinctual life. The punkah-wallah in the court, for example, stands as a sign, to Adela, Forster and the reader, of the profound imperatives beyond immediate, trivial concerns:

he seemed apart from human destinies, a male Fate, a winnower of souls. Opposite him, also on a platform, sat the little Assistant Magistrate, cultivated, self-conscious and conscientious. The punkah-wallah was none of these things; he scarcely knew that he existed and did not understand why the court was fuller than usual, indeed he did not know that it was fuller than usual, didn't even know he worked a fan, though he thought he pulled a rope. Something in his aloofness impressed the girl from middle-class England, and rebuked the narrowness of her sufferings. (p. 221)

In the relationship between Fielding and Aziz, Aziz assumes the familiar Forsterian role of liberating the middle-class Englishman into a life of emotion, but his symbolic spontaneity is contextualized so that his race, religion, personality and class interact with Fielding's unconventionality.

The novel ends famously on the tentative note, ' No, not yet, ... No, not there', a culmination of all Forster's ambivalence about fictional endings. It is worth noting, also, that the structure of the novel is a series of disastrous social encounters – the Bridge Party, Fielding's tea-party, the expedition to the caves – and culminates in the court scene and the Hindu festival. The court scene shows the constraints of human society at its worst; the Hindu festival is an extreme statement of the uncontrollable elements in human and spiritual life. The novel, then, is balanced on two extremes of human communication, but the final congregation is one of reconciliation, when Fielding, Aziz and the others are capsized into the lake. The patterning of the novel into a number of friendships also bears a resemblance to the way relationships are presented in the earlier novels. Aziz becomes friendly with Mrs Moore and Fielding, and disastrously involved with Adela. His fondness for Mrs Moore is intangible, existing more in both their minds than in any particular meetings between them, and Adela disappears two-thirds of the way through the novel. What emerges in the end is the centrality, for Forster, of the relationship between Aziz and Fielding. The conflicts between exclusive heterosexual relationships and male camaraderie, shown in *The Longest Journey* and treated subliminally in *A Room with a View*, are rehearsed once again in *A Passage to India*.

Select Bibliography

Biographical

P. N. Furbank, *E. M. Forster: A Life*, Oxford University Press, 1979.

The Indian context

G. K. Das, *E. M Forster's India*, Macmillan, 1977.

Allen J. Greenberger, *The British Image of India: A Study in the Literature of Imperialism 1880–1960*, Oxford University Press, 1969.

Benita Parry, *Delusions and Discoveries: Studies on India in the British Imagination 1880–1930*, Allen Lane, 1972.

Books on Forster or containing important discussions of 'A Passage to India'

J. W. Beer, *The Achievement of E. M. Forster*, Chatto and Windus, 1962.

Malcolm Bradbury (ed.), *E. M. Forster: 'A Passage to India': A Casebook*, Macmillan, 1970.

John Colmer, *E. M. Forster: The Personal Voice*, Routledge and Kegan Paul, 1975.

F. C. Crews, *E. M. Forster: The Perils of Humanism*, Oxford University Press, 1962.

Philip Gardner (ed.), *E. M. Forster: The Critical Heritage*, Routledge and Kegan Paul, 1973.

Christopher Gillie, *A Preface to Forster*, Longman, 1983.

June Perry Levine, *Creation and Criticism: 'A Passage to India'*, Chatto and Windus, 1971

John Sayre Martin, *E. M. Forster: The Endless Journey*, Cambridge University Press, 1976.

Andrew Rutherford (ed.), *Twentieth-Century Interpretations of 'A Passage to India'*, Prentice-Hall, 1970.

O. Stallybrass (ed.), *Aspects of E. M. Forster*, Edward Arnold, 1969.

Wilfred Stone, *The Cave and the Mountain*, Oxford University Press, 1966.

Lionel Trilling, *E. M. Forster*, Hogarth Press, 1944.

Peter Widdowson, *E. M. Forster's 'Howards End': Fiction as History*, Sussex University Press, 1977.

MORE ABOUT PENGUINS, PELICANS, PEREGRINES AND PUFFINS

For further information about books available from Penguins please write to Dept EP, Penguin Books Ltd, Harmondsworth, Middlesex UB7 0DA.

In the U.S.A.: For a complete list of books available from Penguins in the United States write to Dept DG, Penguin Books, 299 Murray Hill Parkway, East Rutherford, New Jersey 07073.

In Canada: For a complete list of books available from Penguins in Canada write to Penguin Books Canada Limited, 2801 John Street, Markham, Ontario L3R 1B4.

In Australia: For a complete list of books available from Penguins in Australia write to the Marketing Department, Penguin Books Australia Ltd, P.O. Box 257, Ringwood, Victoria 3134.

In New Zealand: For a complete list of books available from Penguins in New Zealand write to the Marketing Department, Penguin Books (N.Z.) Ltd, Private Bag, Takapuna, Auckland 9.

In India: For a complete list of books available from Penguins in India write to Penguin Overseas Ltd, 706 Eros Apartments, 56 Nehru Place, New Delhi 110019.

ENGLISH AND AMERICAN LITERATURE IN PENGUINS

☐ **Emma** Jane Austen £1.25

'I am going to take a heroine whom no one but myself will much like,' declared Jane Austen of Emma, her most spirited and controversial heroine in a comedy of self-deceit and self-discovery.

☐ **Tender is the Night** F. Scott Fitzgerald £2.95

Fitzgerald worked on seventeen different versions of this novel, and its obsessions – idealism, beauty, dissipation, alcohol and insanity – were those that consumed his own marriage and his life.

☐ **The Life of Johnson** James Boswell £2.95

Full of gusto, imagination, conversation and wit, Boswell's immortal portrait of Johnson is as near a novel as a true biography can be, and still regarded by many as the finest 'life' ever written. This shortened version is based on the 1799 edition.

☐ **A House and its Head** Ivy Compton-Burnett £4.95

In a novel 'as trim and tidy as a hand-grenade' (as Pamela Hansford Johnson put it), Ivy Compton-Burnett penetrates the facade of a conventional, upper-class Victorian family to uncover a chasm of violent emotions – jealousy, pain, frustration and sexual passion.

☐ **The Trumpet Major** Thomas Hardy £1.50

Although a vein of unhappy unrequited love runs through this novel, Hardy also draws on his warmest sense of humour to portray Wessex village life at the time of the Napoleonic wars.

☐ **The Complete Poems of Hugh MacDiarmid**
☐ Volume One £8.95
☐ Volume Two £8.95
The definitive edition of work by the greatest Scottish poet since Robert Burns, edited by his son Michael Grieve, and W. R. Aitken.

ENGLISH AND AMERICAN
LITERATURE IN PENGUINS

☐ **Main Street** Sinclair Lewis £4.95

The novel that added an immortal chapter to the literature of America's Mid-West, *Main Street* contains the comic essence of Main Streets everywhere.

☐ **The Compleat Angler** Izaak Walton £2.50

A celebration of the countryside, and the superiority of those in 1653, as now, who love *quietnesse, vertue* and, above all, *Angling*. 'No fish, however coarse, could wish for a doughtier champion than Izaak Walton' – Lord Home

☐ **The Portrait of a Lady** Henry James £2.50

'One of the two most brilliant novels in the language', according to F. R. Leavis, James's masterpiece tells the story of a young American heiress, prey to fortune-hunters but not without a will of her own.

☐ **Hangover Square** Patrick Hamilton £3.95

Part love story, part thriller, and set in the publands of London's Earls Court, this novel caught the conversational tone of a whole generation in the uneasy months before the Second World War.

☐ **The Rainbow** D. H. Lawrence £2.50

Written between *Sons and Lovers* and *Women in Love, The Rainbow* covers three generations of Brangwens, a yeoman family living on the borders of Nottinghamshire.

☐ **Vindication of the Rights of Woman**
Mary Wollstonecraft £2.95

Although Walpole once called her 'a hyena in petticoats', Mary Wollstonecraft's vision was such that modern feminists continue to go back and debate the arguments so powerfully set down here.

CLASSICS IN TRANSLATION
IN PENGUINS

☐ *Remembrance of Things Past* **Marcel Proust**

☐ Volume One: *Swann's Way, Within a Budding Grove*   £7.95
☐ Volume Two: *The Guermantes Way, Cities of the Plain*   £7.95
☐ Volume Three: *The Captive, The Fugitive, Time Regained*   £7.95

Terence Kilmartin's acclaimed revised version of C. K. Scott Moncrieff's original translation, published in paperback for the first time.

☐ *The Canterbury Tales* **Geoffrey Chaucer**   £2.95

'Every age is a Canterbury Pilgrimage . . . nor can a child be born who is not one of these characters of Chaucer' – William Blake

☐ *Gargantua & Pantagruel* **Rabelais**   £3.95

The fantastic adventures of two giants through which Rabelais (1495–1553) caricatured his life and times in a masterpiece of exuberance and glorious exaggeration.

☐ *The Brothers Karamazov* **Fyodor Dostoevsky**   £4.95

A detective story on many levels, profoundly involving the question of the existence of God, Dostoevsky's great drama of parricide and fraternal jealousy triumphantly fulfilled his aim: 'to find the man in man . . . [to] depict all the depths of the human soul.'

☐ *Fables of Aesop*   £1.95

This translation recovers all the old magic of fables in which, too often, the fox steps forward as the cynical hero and a lamb is an ass to lie down with a lion.

☐ *The Three Theban Plays* **Sophocles** .   £2.95

A new translation, by Robert Fagles, of *Antigone, Oedipus the King* and *Oedipus at Colonus*, plays all based on the legend of the royal house of Thebes.

CLASSICS IN TRANSLATION
IN PENGUINS

☐ **The Treasure of the City of Ladies**
   Christine de Pisan   £2.95

This practical survival handbook for women (whether royal courtiers
or prostitutes) paints a vivid picture of their lives and preoccupations
in France, *c*. 1405. First English translation.

☐ **La Regenta** **Leopoldo Alas**   £10.95

This first English translation of this Spanish masterpiece has been
acclaimed as 'a major literary event' – *Observer*. 'Among the select
band of "world novels" ... outstandingly well translated' – John
Bayley in the *Listener*

☐ **Metamorphoses** **Ovid**   £2.95

The whole of Western literature has found inspiration in Ovid's
poem, a golden treasury of myths and legends that are linked by the
theme of transformation.

☐ **Darkness at Noon**   **Arthur Koestler**   £2.50

'Koestler approaches the problem of ends and means, of love and
truth and social organization, through the thoughts of an Old Bolshe-
vik, Rubashov, as he awaits death in a G.P.U. prison' – *New Statesman*

☐ **War and Peace** **Leo Tolstoy**   £4.95

'A complete picture of human life;' wrote one critic, 'a complete
picture of the Russia of that day; a complete picture of everything in
which people place their happiness and greatness, their grief and
humiliation.'

☐ **The Divine Comedy: 1 Hell** **Dante**   £2.25

A new translation by Mark Musa, in which the poet is conducted by
the spirit of Virgil down through the twenty-four closely described
circles of hell.

Penguin Masterstudies

This comprehensive list, designed to help advanced level and undergraduate studies, includes:

Subjects

Applied Mathematics
Biology
Drama: Text into Performance
Geography
Pure Mathematics

Literature

Dr Faustus
Eugenie Grandet
The Great Gatsby
The Mill on the Floss
Persuasion
Portrait of a Lady
Tender Is the Night
Vanity Fair
The Waste Land

Chaucer

The Knight's Tale
The Miller's Tale
The Nun's Priest's Tale
The Pardoner's Tale
The Prologue to The Canterbury Tales
A Chaucer Handbook

Shakespeare

Hamlet
King Lear
Measure for Measure
Othello
The Tempest
A Shakespeare Handbook